Groovy Programming Language for Chatbots

The Ultimate Guide to Building Intelligent Chatbots with Ease

Davis Simon

1

Discover Other Books in the Series

"Groovy Programming Language for Beginners: Your First Steps into Coding"

"Groovy Programming Language for Backend Development:Discover How Groovy Can Revolutionize Your Backend Code"

"Groovy Programming Language for Automation: Unlock the full potential of Groovy to streamline workflows, simplify coding"

"Groovy Programming Language for Data Science: Unlock the Power of Seamless Data Analysis and Automation"

"Groovy Programming Language for Web Development: Building Your First Web App"

"Groovy Programming Language for Big Data:Groovy to Build Scalable, Efficient, and Flexible Big Data Applications"

"Groovy Programming Language for Data Manipulation: Master the Basics and Unlock Advanced Techniques for Game-Changing Results"

"Groovy Programming Language for DevSecOps: Agile Scripting to Secure and Streamline Software Delivery With Groovy"

Disclaimer

The Book titled *" Groovy Programming language for Chatbots:The Ultimate Guide to Building Intelligent Chatbots with Ease"* by Davis Simon is intended for educational and informational purposes only.

The content provided in this eBook is based on the author's experience, research, and personal opinions. It is designed to offer insights and techniques for backend development using the Groovy programming language.

Introduction

Welcome to "**Groovy Programming Language for Chatbots: The Ultimate Guide to Building Intelligent Chatbots with Ease**." In the current digital era, where communication methods have rapidly transformed, chatbots have become indispensable tools for both businesses and developers. They not only facilitate customer interactions but also improve user experiences, rendering them essential assets across various sectors.

As the need for advanced, user-friendly, and interactive chatbots continues to grow, so does the requirement for a robust yet user-friendly programming language to develop them. Groovy emerges as a dynamic language that integrates effortlessly with Java, capitalizing on its strengths and enabling the swift development of intricate applications. With its clear syntax and adaptable paradigms, Groovy is particularly well-equipped for creating intelligent chatbots that can respond to a wide range of user requirements and interactions.

In this detailed guide, we will embark on an engaging exploration of Groovy and its relevance in developing chatbots that are not only effective but also captivating. Whether you are an experienced developer seeking to broaden your skill set or a beginner eager to explore the realm of programming, this book will equip you with the knowledge and expertise to leverage the capabilities of Groovy.We will begin by understanding the fundamentals of the Groovy programming language, exploring its key features and advantages that make it a perfect fit for chatbot development. Next, we will delve into practical applications, from basic chatbot functionalities to advanced conversational AI techniques, including natural language processing (NLP) and machine learning (ML).

Moreover, this guide will be packed with hands-on examples and real-world projects that will empower you to build your own chatbots with ease. You'll learn how to integrate APIs, manage user input, and implement decision-making processes that will help your chatbot understand and respond to users effectively.

By the end of this journey, you will not only have a solid grasp of Groovy but also the confidence to create intelligent chatbots that can enhance customer engagement and solve real problems in innovative ways. Let's unlock the potential of Groovy together and take the first steps toward building chatbots that are not just functional, but truly smart.

Join us as we explore the intersection of Groovy programming and chatbot technology—a combination that has the potential to revolutionize how we interact with machines. Your adventure in building intelligent chatbots begins here!

Chapter 1: Introduction to Groovy for Chatbot Development

Groovy is a dynamic and agile programming language designed for the Java Virtual Machine (JVM). It merges the well-known syntax of Java with a variety of robust features that enhance productivity and minimize boilerplate code. As an object-oriented language, Groovy facilitates a seamless transition for developers moving from Java, allowing them to utilize existing Java libraries and frameworks with ease. Its succinct syntax and dynamic characteristics render Groovy particularly attractive for rapid application development and scripting endeavors.

A key benefit of Groovy lies in its ability to integrate seamlessly with current Java codebases, enabling developers to utilize and expand upon Java libraries without the need for extensive modifications. Additionally, Groovy's advanced metaprogramming capabilities significantly boost developer productivity, making it an excellent choice for diverse applications, including the development of chatbots.

1.2 The Emergence of Chatbots

In recent years, chatbots have transformed the manner in which businesses engage with their customers. Thanks to advancements in artificial intelligence, natural language processing, and machine learning, chatbots have evolved into highly sophisticated tools capable of delivering personalized customer experiences. They fulfill a variety of roles, from addressing customer inquiries and automating repetitive tasks to offering recommendations and collecting feedback.The demand for effective chatbots continues to grow as organizations strive to enhance customer engagement while reducing operational costs. As a result, developers are increasingly looking for tools and languages that enable them to build scalable, efficient, and user-friendly chatbots. Groovy, with its dynamic features and seamless integration with Java, is an excellent choice for this purpose.

1.3 Why Choose Groovy for Chatbot Development?
1.3.1 Concise and Readable Syntax

One of the defining features of Groovy is its clean and concise syntax, which allows developers to write less code while accomplishing more. This readability is particularly important when building chatbots, where maintaining and updating code efficiently is crucial.

1.3.2 Dynamic Typing and Scripting Capabilities

Groovy's dynamic typing eliminates the need for boilerplate code often associated with statically typed languages like Java. Developers can write scripts that dynamically bind to data types at runtime, enabling rapid prototyping and development. This feature is invaluable for chatbot development, where quick iteration and testing of conversational logic can significantly shorten the development lifecycle.

1.3.3 Seamless Integration with Java Ecosystem

Since Groovy is built on the Java platform, it can utilize the vast ecosystem of Java libraries and frameworks, such as Spring, Hibernate, and Apache Camel. By harnessing these libraries, developers can create powerful chatbots with features like rich natural language processing (NLP) capabilities, database access, and web service integration.

1.3.4 Groovy and Frameworks for Chatbot Development

Several frameworks, such as Grails and Micronaut, leverage Groovy to streamline the development of web applications, including chatbots. These frameworks often come equipped with built-in tools and plugins that enhance productivity and simplify common tasks.

1.3.5 Community Support and Growing Popularity

The Groovy community is vibrant and active, providing a wealth of resources, tutorials, and plugins. As Groovy continues to gain traction within the development community, the availability of libraries and frameworks tailored to chatbot development expands, making it easier for developers to find the tools they need.

1.4 Overview of This Book

This book is designed to serve as a comprehensive guide for developers wanting to use Groovy to create powerful chatbots. It will take you through the essential concepts, tools, and best practices for effective chatbot development using Groovy.

Chapter breakdown:

Chapter 2: Setting Up the Development Environment – Learn how to install Groovy and set up your preferred IDE for chatbot development.

Chapter 3: Groovy Language Fundamentals – Explore Groovy's core language features, including syntax, closures, collections, and more.

Chapter 4: Introduction to Chatbot Architectures –

Understand the various architectures and designs commonly used in chatbot development.

Chapter 5: Integrating Natural Language Processing – Discover how to implement NLP capabilities in your chatbots using Groovy.

Chapter 6: Building a Simple Chatbot – Follow a step-by-step guide to building your first chatbot application.

Chapter 7: Testing and Debugging Chatbots – Learn useful techniques for testing and debugging your chatbot effectively.

Chapter 8: Deploying Your Chatbot – Explore deployment options and best practices for making your chatbot available to users.

Chapter 9: Advanced Chatbot Features – Delve into advanced techniques, including integrating with third-party APIs and enhancing user experience.

The combination of Groovy's elegance and the growing demand for chatbots presents a unique opportunity for developers to excel in this exciting field. Prepare to dive deeper into the mechanics of Groovy and discover how to leverage its full potential to bring your chatbot ideas to life!

The Power Groovy Programming for Chatbots

Automating conversations allows organizations to improve efficiency, provide instant support, and enhance user experience. While several programming languages are available for chatbot development, Groovy stands out due to its simplicity, flexibility, and powerful features.

This chapter delves into the advantages of using Groovy for chatbot programming, explores its ecosystem, and provides practical examples to illustrate its benefits.

Why Groovy?

1. **Simplicity and Conciseness**

Groovy, a dynamic language that runs on the Java platform, is known for its human-readable syntax. This ease of use is especially beneficial for developers who are new to programming or those familiar only with Java. By reducing boilerplate code, Groovy enables developers to focus more on the logic of the chatbot rather than the intricacies of syntax.

2. **Seamless Integration with Java**

One of Groovy's key strengths is its seamless integration with Java. As a JVM language, Groovy can leverage existing Java libraries and frameworks, allowing developers to access a rich ecosystem without reinventing the wheel. This feature is particularly advantageous when incorporating more complex functionalities, such as natural language processing (NLP) or machine learning algorithms.

3. **Dynamic Features**

Groovy offers dynamic typing, which can significantly accelerate the development process. Developers can write flexible and dynamic code that can adapt to changing requirements with minimal effort. This dynamism is particularly valuable in an agile environment where chatbot functionalities may need to be adjusted frequently based on user feedback and analytics.

4. **Powerful Scripting Capabilities**

Chatbots often require rapid prototyping and quick iterations. Groovy shines in scripting scenarios, allowing developers to quickly write and test their code in real time. This capability ensures that feedback loops are efficient, reducing the time taken to deploy updates and new features.

Groovy Libraries for Chatbot Development

The Groovy ecosystem is abundant with libraries that serve various chatbot-related functionalities. Let's explore some notable ones:

1. **Grails**

Grails is a web application framework that leverages Groovy and follows the "convention over configuration" principle. It simplifies the development of web applications, including chatbots, featuring rapid development capabilities, built-in scaffolding, and powerful plugins. Using Grails, developers can quickly set up a web server that can handle incoming chatbot requests and responds to users efficiently.

2. **Natural Language Processing Libraries**

Integrating natural language understanding in chatbots can greatly enhance their capabilities. Libraries like

Stanford NLP or **OpenNLP** can be easily incorporated into Groovy applications, enabling developers to analyze user inputs effectively. Using these libraries, you can build chatbots that understand context, detect intents, and respond intelligently.

3. **WebSocket and RESTful Services**

Groovy supports various ways to interact with users,

14

including RESTful APIs and WebSockets. Utilizing libraries like **Ratpack** or the built-in Groovy HTTP capabilities, you can develop real-time communication features, allowing the chatbot to maintain a persistent connection with users and provide immediate feedback.

Building a Simple Chatbot with Groovy

To illustrate the effectiveness of Groovy in chatbot development, let's walk through creating a simple command-line chatbot.

Step 1: Setting Up Groovy Environment

Ensure Groovy is installed and set up on your machine. You can do this by downloading the latest version from the [Groovy website](https://groovy-lang.org). Once installed, you can use the command line to run Groovy scripts.

Step 2: Basic Chatbot Structure

Create a new Groovy file named `SimpleChatbot.groovy`:

```groovy
class SimpleChatbot {

def greetings = [

"hello": "Hi there! How can I help you today?", "bye": "Goodbye! Have a great day!"

]

def respond(String input) {

def response = greetings[input.toLowerCase()] return response ?: "I'm sorry, I don't understand."

}
```

15

```groovy
def startChat() {

println "Welcome to the Simple Chatbot!" println "Type
'bye' to exit."

while (true) { print "You: "

def userInput = System.console().readLine()

if (userInput.toLowerCase() == "bye") { println
respond("bye")

break

}

println "Chatbot: " + respond(userInput)

}

}

}

def chatbot = new SimpleChatbot() chatbot.startChat()
```
```

### **Step 3: Running the Bot**

You can run this script by executing the following
command in your terminal:

```bash
groovy SimpleChatbot.groovy
```

You will be welcomed by the chatbot, and you can start
typing your messages. The bot will respond based on the
defined greetings or indicate it doesn't understand.

Groovy's capabilities make it a powerful language for
```

developing chatbots. Its simplicity, robust ecosystem, and dynamic features enable developers to create efficient and flexible chatbot applications. As the demand for intelligent conversational agents continues to grow, Groovy provides the tools necessary to engage users meaningfully and efficiently. Whether you are building a simple Q&A bot or a more complex conversational agent, embracing Groovy can enhance your development experience and lead to outstanding results.

Chatbot Development in Groovy Fundamentals

This chapter will explore how to leverage Groovy, a powerful dynamic language for the Java platform, to develop efficient and effective chatbots. We will cover the fundamental aspects of Groovy, discuss its advantages for chatbot development, and walk through a simple implementation to get you started.

1. Understanding Groovy

Before diving into chatbot development, it's essential to have a grasp of what Groovy is and why it's suitable for this purpose.

1.1 What is Groovy?

Groovy is an agile, dynamic language that complements Java. It combines the familiarity of Java syntax with powerful features such as closures, dynamic typing, and the ability to directly integrate with existing Java libraries. It encourages concise code, making it an appealing option for rapid application development.

1.2 Advantages of Groovy for Chatbot Development

Simplicity and Conciseness: Groovy's syntax is less verbose than Java, allowing developers to write more straightforward and maintainable code.

Seamless Integration: As Groovy runs on the Java Virtual Machine (JVM), it can easily interact with Java libraries, which is advantageous for leveraging existing tools and frameworks in chatbot development.

Dynamic Typing: With dynamic typing, Groovy allows for more flexibility during development, enabling quick iterations and testing.

Built-in Features: Groovy includes powerful features such as closures and meta-programming that can enhance chatbot behavior and capabilities.

2. Setting Up Your Groovy Environment

To start developing a chatbot in Groovy, you need to set up your development environment. Follow these steps:

2.1 Install Groovy

Download Groovy: Visit the [Apache Groovy website](https://groovy.apache.org/download.html) and download the latest version.

Install Groovy: Follow the installation instructions for your operating system. Ensure that Groovy's bin directory is added to your system's PATH variable.

Verify Installation: Open your terminal or command prompt and type:

```bash
```

```groovy
groovy -version
```
```

This command should display the Groovy version installed on your system. ### 2.2 Setting Up an IDE

It's recommended to use an Integrated Development Environment (IDE) that supports Groovy. IntelliJ IDEA and Eclipse with the Groovy plugin are popular choices. Install either and create a new Groovy project to start implementing your chatbot.

## 3. Building a Simple Chatbot

### 3.1 Defining the Chatbot Structure

A basic chatbot should have the following components:

**Input Handler**: For processing user input.

**Response Generator**: To formulate appropriate replies based on user input.

**Conversation Logic**: The flow of the conversation, managing context and state. ### 3.2 Implementing the Chatbot

Let's create a simple CLI-based chatbot in Groovy. This chatbot will respond to greetings and provide information about the weather.

```groovy
class SimpleChatbot {

def start() {

println "Welcome to Groovy Chatbot! Type 'exit' to end the chat."
```
```

```
while (true) { print "You: "
def userInput = System.console().readLine()
if (userInput.equalsIgnoreCase("exit")) { println "Chatbot:
Goodbye!"
break
}
respond(userInput)
}
}
def respond(String input) {
if           (input.equalsIgnoreCase("hello")           ||
input.equalsIgnoreCase("hi")) { println "Chatbot: Hello!
How can I assist you today?"
} else if (input.equalsIgnoreCase("what's the weather?")) {
println "Chatbot: Currently, it's sunny and 75°F."
} else {
println "Chatbot: I'm sorry, I don't understand that."
}
}
static     void     main(String[]     args)     {     new
SimpleChatbot().start()
}
}
```
```
```

3.3 Running the Chatbot

Copy the code above into a new Groovy file named `SimpleChatbot.groovy`.

Open your terminal, navigate to the project directory, and run:

```bash
groovy SimpleChatbot.groovy
```

3.4 Interacting with the Chatbot

Once the chatbot is running, users can start typing messages. The chatbot will respond based on predefined rules, demonstrating how you can initiate conversation and provide basic responses.

4. Expanding Chatbot Functionality

With the fundamentals in place, you can enhance your chatbot in various ways: ### 4.1 Utilizing API Integrations

You can integrate APIs to fetch real-time data, like weather updates or news. For example, you might use the OpenWeatherMap API to provide accurate weather information based on user location.

4.2 Natural Language Processing (NLP)

For more advanced user interaction, consider incorporating NLP libraries like Stanford NLP or Apache OpenNLP. These tools can improve understanding of user queries and enhance response accuracy.

4.3 State Management

To manage more complex conversations, implement state management. You could maintain user context, which allows the chatbot to remember information between interactions.

We discussed the advantages of using Groovy for this purpose, set up our development environment, and built a simple chatbot to showcase basic functionalities. As you delve deeper into chatbot development, consider exploring integrations, NLP, and state management to create a more sophisticated and responsive user experience. The world of chatbots is vast and offers exciting opportunities for innovation—let your creativity guide you as you build your next intelligent application!

Chapter 2: Setting Up Your Development Environment

In this chapter, we will delve into the prerequisites and step-by-step procedures to set up an efficient development environment for Groovy, allowing you to focus on coding, design patterns, and all the exciting features Groovy has to offer.

2.1 Understanding Groovy

Before we dive into the setup process, it's essential to understand what Groovy is. Groovy is an agile and dynamic language for the Java Virtual Machine (JVM), designed to enhance developer productivity by offering a concise, expressive syntax while being fully interoperable with Java. Being a scripting language, Groovy is often embraced for building applications, automating tasks, and enhancing existing Java codebases.

2.2 Prerequisites

2.2.1 Java Development Kit (JDK)

Since Groovy runs on the JVM, the first element of our environment is the Java Development Kit (JDK). You will need to install a compatible JDK to run Groovy. Here are the typical steps to install the JDK:

Download the JDK: Visit the official Oracle website or OpenJDK's website to download the latest version of the JDK. Choose the installation package that is appropriate for your operating system.

Install the JDK: Follow the installation instructions

specific to your OS. Make note of the installation path, as you may need it later.

Set Environment Variables:

Windows: Set the `JAVA_HOME` variable to the path of your JDK installation. Add

`JAVA_HOME/bin` to your `PATH` variable.

Mac/Linux: You can set the `JAVA_HOME` in your shell configuration file (e.g., `.bash_profile`,

`.bashrc`, or `.zshrc`).

To verify that your JDK is installed correctly, run `java -version` in your terminal or command prompt:

```bash
java -version
```

2.2.2 Groovy Installation

With the JDK set up, the next step is to install Groovy. Let's explore the options for installing Groovy on your machine.

Using SDKMAN!:

SDKMAN! is a great tool for managing parallel versions of multiple Software Development Kits, including Groovy.

Open a terminal and install SDKMAN!:

```bash
curl -s "https://get.sdkman.io" | bash
```

```
```

Then, follow the instructions displayed in your terminal to initialize SDKMAN!

Install Groovy:

```bash
sdk install groovy
```

Manual Installation:

If you prefer to install Groovy manually:

Download the latest distribution from Groovy's official website: [Groovy Downloads](https://groovy-lang.org/download.html).

Extract the files to a directory, such as `/opt/groovy` (Linux) or `C:\Groovy` (Windows).

Set the `GROOVY_HOME` environment variable to the path where Groovy is installed, and add

`GROOVY_HOME/bin` to your `PATH`.

To verify Groovy installation, run:

```bash
groovy --version
```

2.2.3 Integrated Development Environment (IDE)

While you can write Groovy code in any text editor, using an IDE can significantly enhance your development experience. Here are a few popular options:

IntelliJ IDEA: A feature-rich IDE that offers excellent support for Groovy and is perfect for Java developers, as it seamlessly integrates with Java projects.

Eclipse with Groovy Plugin: Eclipse, another popular IDE, can be equipped with a Groovy plugin for development support.

VSCode: With the Groovy extension, Visual Studio Code becomes a lightweight yet capable environment for Groovy development.

After choosing an IDE, download and follow the installation instructions for your operating system. Once installed, set up a new project, select Groovy as your language, and configure the JDK if prompted.

2.3 Creating Your First Groovy Script

Now that your development environment is ready, let's write your first Groovy script to test your setup:

Create a new Groovy file: Open your IDE, create a new file named `HelloWorld.groovy`.

Write a simple Groovy script:

```groovy
println 'Hello, World!'
```

Run your script:

- From the terminal, navigate to the directory containing your script and execute:

```bash
```

```
groovy HelloWorld.groovy
```
` ` `

- If everything is set up correctly, you should see the output `Hello, World!` printed in your console.

In this chapter, we covered the essential steps required to set up a development environment for Groovy, from installing the JDK and Groovy itself to choosing an IDE. With your environment correctly configured, you are now ready to explore Groovy's numerous features, libraries, and frameworks. In the following chapters, we will dive deeper into Groovy's syntax, key concepts, and practical applications that make it a favorite among developers. Happy coding!

Installing Groovy and Essential Tools

This chapter will guide you through the installation of Groovy and the essential tools required to kickstart your chatbot development journey.

1. Understanding Groovy

Before diving into the installation process, let's take a moment to understand what Groovy is and why it's a suitable choice for building chatbots. Groovy is an agile and versatile programming language that runs on the Java Virtual Machine (JVM). Its seamless integration with Java allows developers to leverage existing Java libraries while enjoying a more concise and expressive syntax. Additionally, Groovy supports dynamic typing, closure, and other modern programming paradigms, making it an ideal choice for rapid application development, including chatbots.

2. Prerequisites

Before installing Groovy and the necessary tools, ensure that you have the following prerequisites on your system:

Java Development Kit (JDK): Groovy is built on top of Java, so you need the JDK installed on your machine. You can download the latest version from the [Oracle website](https://www.oracle.com/java/technologies/java se-jdk11-downloads.html) or use OpenJDK, which is available in many package managers.

A suitable IDE: While you can use any text editor to write Groovy code, an Integrated Development Environment (IDE) can enhance your coding experience. Popular choices include:

IntelliJ IDEA (Community Edition)

Eclipse with the Groovy plugin

Visual Studio Code with Groovy extensions

A terminal/command prompt: Familiarity with the command line will be beneficial for executing commands and scripts.

3. Installing Groovy

3.1. Method 1: Using SDKMAN!

One of the simplest ways to install Groovy is by using SDKMAN!, a tool for managing parallel versions of multiple Software Development Kits on most Unix-based systems.

Step 1: Install SDKMAN!

Open a terminal and run the following command:

```bash
curl -s "https://get.sdkman.io" | bash
```

Follow the on-screen instructions to complete the installation. Once installed, you may need to restart your terminal or run:

```bash
source "$HOME/.sdkman/bin/sdkman-init.sh"
```

Step 2: Install Groovy

Once SDKMAN! is properly set up, you can install Groovy by executing:

```bash
sdk install groovy
```

You can verify the installation by checking the version:

```bash
groovy -version
```

3.2. Method 2: Manual Installation

If you prefer to install Groovy manually, follow these steps:

Step 1: Download Groovy

Visit the official Groovy website at [groovy-lang.org](https://groovy-lang.org/download.html) and download the latest distribution archive (ZIP or TAR.GZ) suitable for your operating system.

Step 2: Extract the Archive

Extract the downloaded archive to your desired location. For example:

```bash
tar -xvzf groovy-all-X.X.X.zip -C /opt/
```

Step 3: Set Environment Variables

You need to set the `GROOVY_HOME` environment variable to point to the Groovy installation directory, and update your `PATH` variable. Add the following lines to your shell configuration file (e.g., `.bashrc`, `.bash_profile`, `.zshrc`):

```bash
export GROOVY_HOME=/opt/groovy-<version> export PATH=$PATH:$GROOVY_HOME/bin
```

After adding these lines, run:

```bash
source ~/.bashrc  # or the relevant file for your shell
```

Step 4: Verify Installation Check the installation by

running:

```bash
groovy -version
```

4. Essential Tools for Chatbot Development

Now that Groovy is installed, let's explore the essential tools for chatbot development.

4.1. Communication Protocols

For a chatbot to communicate effectively with users, understanding communication protocols is crucial. Popular protocols include:

HTTP/REST: Many chatbots use REST APIs to communicate with external services. You can utilize the built-in HTTP capabilities of Groovy and libraries such as `HTTPBuilder`.

WebSockets: For real-time communication, consider using WebSocket connections. Libraries like

`Groovy WebSocket` can simplify this process. ### 4.2. Frameworks and Libraries

Several frameworks and libraries can enhance your chatbot development experience:

Grails: A web application framework that is built on Groovy, Grails provides a productive environment for creating modern web applications, including chatbots.

Bot Frameworks: Consider using frameworks like Rasa or Dialogflow for natural language processing (NLP)

capabilities. These frameworks support integration with Groovy, allowing for powerful chatbot interactions.

4.3. Testing Tools

To ensure that your chatbot is functioning correctly, you will need testing tools:

Spock: A testing and specification framework for Java and Groovy applications. It allows easy writing of tests for your Groovy chatbot code.

Postman: A versatile tool for testing APIs that can be beneficial for testing chatbot responses and interactions through REST APIs.

4.4. Version Control

Lastly, utilize version control systems like Git to keep track of your chatbot development process. Platforms like GitHub and GitLab offer collaborative features that are essential for team-based projects.

With Groovy's powerful features and the right tools at your disposal, you are well on your way to creating engaging and intelligent chatbots that can enhance user interactions in various applications. As you progress, remember to experiment and explore the extensive libraries and frameworks available in the Groovy ecosystem, which will allow you to take your chatbot projects to the next level.

Creating Your First Groovy Script

Groovy is an agile and dynamic language for the Java

platform that combines powerful features of Python, Ruby, and Smalltalk with the strengths of Java. It offers seamless integration with Java, a concise syntax, and the flexibility to adapt to different programming paradigms. Its ability to simplify the Java development process has made Groovy a popular choice for scripting, testing, and building domain-specific languages (DSLs).

In this chapter, we will guide you through the process of creating your first Groovy script. We will cover the essential basics of setting up your environment, writing a simple script, executing it, and understanding the core syntax and structure of Groovy code.

Setting Up Your Environment

Before we can dive into scripting, we need to set up our development environment. Specifically, we need to have Groovy installed on our machine. Here's how you can do that:

Step 1: Install Java

Groovy runs on the Java platform, so you need to have a Java Development Kit (JDK) installed. You can download the latest version from the [Oracle website](https://www.oracle.com/java/technologies/java se- downloads.html) or use OpenJDK.

Step 2: Install Groovy

Groovy can be installed in several ways. The easiest option is to install it using SDKMAN, a tool for managing parallel versions of Software Development Kits. To install SDKMAN:

Open your terminal and run the following command:

```bash
curl -s "https://get.sdkman.io" | bash
```

Follow the instructions in your terminal to finalize the installation.

Once SDKMAN is installed, you can install Groovy by running:

```bash
sdk install groovy
```

Step 3: Verify the Installation

After installation, verify that Groovy is installed correctly by executing:

```bash
groovy -version
```

You should see the version number of Groovy printed in the terminal.

Writing Your First Groovy Script

Now that we have Groovy set up, let's create our first Groovy script. Groovy scripts can be written in any text editor, but using a dedicated IDE like IntelliJ IDEA or Eclipse with Groovy support can make development easier.

Step 1: Create a New File

Open your text editor or IDE and create a new file named `HelloWorld.groovy`. ### Step 2: Write the Script

In `HelloWorld.groovy`, write the following code:

```groovy
println 'Hello, World!'
```

This simple script uses the `println` method to output the text "Hello, World!" to the console. ## Executing Your Groovy Script

Now that we have our script ready, it's time to execute it. To run your Groovy script, follow these steps: ### Step 1: Open Terminal

Navigate to the directory where your `HelloWorld.groovy` file is saved using the terminal. ### Step 2: Run the Script

Execute the script by entering the following command:

```bash
groovy HelloWorld.groovy
```

Step 3: See the Output

If everything is set up correctly, you should see the following output:

```
Hello, World!
```

Congratulations! You've successfully created and executed your first Groovy script. ## Understanding Basic Groovy

Syntax

Now that you've created and run a simple script, let's explore some basic Groovy syntax and features: ### Variables

In Groovy, you can declare variables without explicitly defining their types. For example:

```groovy
def message = 'Hello, Groovy!'


println message
```

The `def` keyword is used to declare a variable, and you can perform various operations without worrying about data types.

Lists and Maps

Groovy provides intuitive ways to handle lists and maps. Here's how you can create and manipulate them:

```groovy
def myList = [1, 2, 3, 4]

myList.each { println it }  // Iterate over the list

def myMap = [name: 'Groovy', version: '3.0']

println "Language: ${myMap.name}, Version: ${myMap.version}"
```

Closures

36

Closures are a powerful feature in Groovy, allowing you to encapsulate code blocks and pass them around. For example:

```groovy
def greet = { name -> println "Hello, $name!"
}

greet('Student') // Outputs: Hello, Student!
```

In this chapter, you learned how to set up your Groovy environment, write your first script, and understand some basic syntax and features. Groovy's dynamic and flexible nature makes it a powerful tool for developers, and mastering it opens the door to many possibilities in software development.

Chapter 3: Groovy Fundamentals for Chatbot Developers

These digital conversational agents can assist users in countless ways, from providing customer support to delivering personalized recommendations. To create effective chatbots, developers are increasingly turning to Groovy, a powerful and flexible programming language that integrates seamlessly with the Java platform. In this chapter, we will explore the fundamental concepts and features of Groovy that make it an excellent choice for chatbot development.

3.1 Introduction to Groovy

Groovy is an object-oriented programming language that runs on the Java Virtual Machine (JVM). It is dynamically typed, which means that variable types are determined at runtime rather than compile-time, giving developers more flexibility. Groovy has a syntax that is concise and easy to read, making it accessible for both new and experienced programmers.

One of the standout features of Groovy is its seamless integration with existing Java code. Developers can leverage Java libraries and frameworks within their Groovy applications, allowing them to build sophisticated chatbots without starting from scratch. This interoperability is particularly advantageous for teams that have prior experience with Java, as they can quickly adapt and expand their skill set to include Groovy.

3.2 Setting Up Your Groovy Environment

Before diving into chatbot development with Groovy, it's essential to set up your development environment. Here's how to get started:

Install the Java Development Kit (JDK): Since Groovy runs on the JVM, you need to have the JDK installed on your machine. Make sure to download the latest version from the [official Oracle website](https://www.oracle.com/java/technologies/javase-jdk11-downloads.html).

Download Groovy: The next step is to download Groovy. You can get the latest version from the [Groovy website](https://groovy-lang.org/download.html). Follow the installation instructions specific to your operating system.

Set Environment Variables: After installation, ensure that the Groovy executable is added to your system's PATH variable. This allows you to run Groovy commands from your command line.

Choose Your IDE: While you can write Groovy code in any text editor, using an Integrated Development Environment (IDE) can significantly enhance your productivity. Popular options include IntelliJ IDEA, Eclipse, and Visual Studio Code, all of which support Groovy development.

With your environment set up, you're ready to start coding. ## 3.3 Groovy Basics

Understanding the core concepts of Groovy is crucial for effective chatbot development. Here are a few fundamental features of Groovy:

3.3.1 Variables and Data Types

In Groovy, you can define variables without specifying their types:

```groovy
def greet = "Hello, Chatbot!" println(greet)
```

Groovy recognizes the type of a variable at runtime based on the assigned value. Common data types include

`String`, `Integer`, `Boolean`, and collections like `List` and `Map`. ### 3.3.2 Control Structures

Groovy supports standard control structures such as `if`, `for`, and `while`. These are critical for managing the flow of your chatbot's logic. For example:

```groovy
def userInput = "hello"
if (userInput == "hello") { println("Hi there!")
} else {
println("I didn't understand that.")
}
```

3.3.3 Closures

Closures are a cornerstone of Groovy's syntax. They are similar to anonymous functions in other languages and can simplify code organization and readability. For instance:

```groovy
def greetUser = { name -> println("Hello, $name!") }
```

```groovy
greetUser("Alice")
```

This feature is particularly useful for callback functions and event handling in chatbots. ## 3.4 Enhanced Handling of JSON

Most chatbots today interact with external services and APIs, often exchanging data in JSON format. Groovy provides excellent built-in support for JSON manipulation, allowing developers to parse and generate JSON effortlessly.

To parse JSON data:

```groovy
import groovy.json.JsonSlurper

def jsonString = '{"name": "Chatbot", "version": "1.0"}' def json = new JsonSlurper().parseText(jsonString) println(json.name) // Output: Chatbot
```

Conversely, to create JSON data:

```groovy
import groovy.json.JsonBuilder

def builder = new JsonBuilder() builder.chatbot {

name "Chatbot" version "1.0"

}

println(builder.toPrettyString())
```

41

3.5 Building a Basic Chatbot

Now that you are familiar with Groovy's fundamental concepts, let's put them into practice by building a simple chatbot. This basic chatbot will respond to user input based on predefined commands.

```groovy
def botResponses = [

"hi": "Hello, how can I assist you today?",

"help": "Here are some things I can help you with: ...",
"bye": "Goodbye! Have a great day!"
]
def chat() {

println("Chatbot: Hi! Type 'bye' to exit.") while (true) {

def userInput = System.console().readLine("You: ")

if (userInput == null || userInput.trim().isEmpty())
continue userInput = userInput.toLowerCase()

if      (botResponses.containsKey(userInput))      {
println("Chatbot: ${botResponses[userInput]}")

} else if (userInput == "bye") { println("Chatbot:
Goodbye!") break

} else {

println("Chatbot: I don't understand that.")

}

}

}
```

chat()
```

In this basic example, the chatbot listens for user input and replies based on predefined commands stored in a map. This design can be further enhanced with complex logic, natural language processing, and integration with external APIs.

Groovy's syntax and versatility make it an ideal language for chatbot development. Its compatibility with Java, combined with features like closures, native JSON handling, and dynamic typing, allows developers to create robust chatbots efficiently. As we move forward in this book, we will build on these fundamentals, exploring more advanced techniques, libraries, and frameworks that will enable you to develop complex conversational agents tailored to your users' needs.

## Key Groovy Syntax and Concepts

Groovy is a powerful and dynamic language built on the Java Virtual Machine (JVM) and designed for ease of use, flexibility, and productivity. As a language that enhances Java, Groovy retains Java's syntax while also incorporating several advanced features that make coding simpler and more intuitive. This chapter delves into the key syntax and concepts of Groovy, enabling you to leverage its potential in your programming projects.

## 1. Groovy Basics: The Essentials ### 1.1. Syntax

Groovy's syntax is designed to be concise and readable. Here are some features that highlight its simplicity:

43
```

- **Semicolon-Free**: Unlike Java, Groovy does not require semicolons at the end of statements, which leads to cleaner and more natural code.

```groovy
def name = "Groovy" println name
```

- **Dynamic Typing**: Groovy is a dynamically typed language, which allows variables to be declared without explicit types. The type is determined at runtime.

```groovy
def age = 25 // age is now an Integer

age = "Twenty-five" // age is now a String
```

- **Optional Parentheses**: In Groovy, parentheses around method arguments are optional, which can enhance readability.

```groovy
println "Hello, world!"

// can also be written as println("Hello, world!")
```

1.2. Closures

A defining feature of Groovy is its support for closures, which are blocks of code that can be assigned to variables, passed as parameters, and executed at a later time.

```groovy
```

```groovy
def greet = { name -> println "Hello, $name!" }
greet("World") // Output: Hello, World!
```

Closures can access variables from their surrounding context (lexical scoping), and they can also define parameters with default values.

```groovy
def add = { a, b -> a + b } println add(2, 3) // Output: 5

def multiply = { a, b = 2 -> a * b } println multiply(4) // Output: 8
```

2. Collections: Lists, Maps, and Arrays

Groovy enhances the traditional Java collections with syntactic sugar that simplifies their use. ### 2.1. Lists

Lists can be created using square brackets, and you can add, remove, or access elements with minimal syntax.

```groovy
def fruits = ["Apple", "Banana", "Cherry"] fruits << "Date" // Add an element

println fruits[2] // Output: Cherry
```

2.2. Maps

Maps in Groovy use a simplified notation, allowing you to create key-value pairs easily.

```groovy
```

```groovy
def person = [name: "Alice", age: 30] println person["name"] // Output: Alice
```

You can also use dot notation for accessing values.

```groovy
println person.age // Output: 30
```

2.3. Ranges

Groovy supports range objects, which can be used in loops or as lists.

```groovy
def range = 1..5
range.each { println it } // Outputs: 1 2 3 4 5
```

3. Control Structures

Groovy inherits control structures from Java but often has more concise options. ### 3.1. Conditional Statements

If-else statements in Groovy retain familiar Java syntax but can also make use of Elvis operator (`?:`).

```groovy
def score = 85
def result = (score > 60) ? "Pass" : "Fail" println result // Output: Pass
```

3.2. Switch Case

Groovy's switch statement is enhanced, allowing for more complex types of matching.

```groovy
def day = "Saturday" switch (day) {

case "Saturday":

case "Sunday":

println "It's the weekend!" break

default:

println "It's a weekday."

}
```

4. Object-Oriented Features

Groovy supports object-oriented programming with classes, inheritance, and interfaces. ### 4.1. Classes and Objects

Defining a class in Groovy is straightforward. It can also have properties and methods.

```groovy
class Person {

String name int age


void introduce() {

println "Hi, I'm $name and I'm $age years old."

}
```

```groovy
}

def alice = new Person(name: "Alice", age: 30)
alice.introduce() // Output: Hi, I'm Alice and I'm 30 years old.
```

4.2. Inheritance

Groovy allows classes to inherit from other classes seamlessly.

```groovy
class Employee extends Person {
String position

void work() {
println "$name is working as a $position."

}
}
```

5. Exception Handling

Exception handling in Groovy is verbose yet succinct, allowing for more straightforward error management.

```groovy
try {
int result = 10 / 0
} catch (ArithmeticException e) {
```

48

```
println "Caught an exception: ${e.message}"
} finally {
println "Execution completed."
}
```
```

From its concise syntax to robust features like closures and dynamic typing, Groovy provides an excellent environment for both scripting and full-fledged application development. By understanding these fundamentals, you can confidently begin your journey into Groovy programming, taking full advantage of its capabilities to create efficient and readable code.

# Object-Oriented Programming in Groovy

This chapter delves into the fundamentals of object-oriented programming in Groovy, exploring its core concepts, features, and practical applications.

## 1. Understanding Objects and Classes

At the heart of OOP lies the concept of objects. An object is an instance of a class, which serves as a blueprint defining the attributes (properties) and behaviors (methods) that the object will possess. In Groovy, creating classes and objects is straightforward, thanks to its simplified and flexible syntax.

### 1.1 Defining a Class

To define a class in Groovy, you use the `class` keyword
```

followed by the class name. Here's an example of a simple class representing a `Car`:

```groovy
class Car {
String make String model int year
void displayInfo() {
println "This car is a ${year} ${make} ${model}."
}
}
```

In this example, `Car` has three properties: `make`, `model`, and `year`, as well as a method `displayInfo()` that prints information about the car.

1.2 Creating an Object

Once a class is defined, you can create instances (objects) of that class. Here's how to create a `Car` object and call its method:

```groovy
def myCar = new Car(make: 'Toyota', model: 'Corolla', year: 2020) myCar.displayInfo() // Output: This car is a 2020 Toyota Corolla.
```

Using named parameters (`make:`, `model:`, `year:`) simplifies object instantiation. ## 2. Inheritance and Polymorphism

One of the key features of OOP is inheritance, which allows a class (the subclass) to derive properties and methods from another class (the superclass). Groovy supports inheritance, enabling code reuse and creating hierarchical class structures.

2.1 Inheritance

Let's extend our `Car` class by creating a subclass named `ElectricCar`:

```groovy
class ElectricCar extends Car { int batteryCapacity // in kWh

void displayInfo() {

super.displayInfo() // Call to the superclass method

println "This electric car has a battery capacity of ${batteryCapacity} kWh."

}

}
```

In this example, `ElectricCar` inherits from `Car`, adding a new property `batteryCapacity` and overriding the `displayInfo()` method to provide additional information.

2.2 Polymorphism

Polymorphism allows objects of different classes to be treated as objects of a common superclass. This is achieved through method overriding. Here's an example of how polymorphism works in Groovy:

```groovy
```

```groovy
def printCarInfo(Car car) { car.displayInfo()
}

def myElectricCar = new ElectricCar(make: 'Tesla', model:
'Model 3', year: 2021, batteryCapacity: 75)
printCarInfo(myElectricCar)  // This will call the
overridden displayInfo() method.
```

In this case, the `printCarInfo()` method accepts a `Car` object, but it can be passed an instance of

`ElectricCar`, demonstrating polymorphism. ## 3. Encapsulation

Encapsulation is another fundamental principle of OOP that involves bundling the data (attributes) and methods (behaviors) that operate on the data into a single unit, or class. It also restricts direct access to some of the object's components, which is a means of preventing unintended interference and misuse of the methods and data.

3.1 Access Modifiers

Groovy provides access modifiers like `public`, `private`, and `protected` to control visibility:

```groovy
class BankAccount { private double balance

void deposit(double amount) { if (amount > 0) {

balance += amount
}
}
```

```groovy
double getBalance() { return balance
}
}
```

In the `BankAccount` class, the `balance` variable is marked as `private`, meaning it cannot be accessed directly from outside the class. The `deposit()` method provides controlled access to modify the balance, while the `getBalance()` method allows retrieval of the balance.

4. Interfaces and Abstract Classes

Groovy also supports interfaces and abstract classes, which are essential for defining contracts and ensuring certain functionalities across different classes.

4.1 Interfaces

An interface defines a contract that implementing classes must adhere to. Here's an example:

```groovy
interface Drivable { void drive()
}
class Bicycle implements Drivable { void drive() {
println "The bicycle is being pedaled."
}
}
```

4.2 Abstract Classes

Abstract classes cannot be instantiated and may contain abstract methods (methods without an implementation). Subclasses must implement these methods:

```groovy
abstract class Shape { abstract double area()
}
class Rectangle extends Shape { double width
double height
double area() {
return width * height
}
}
```

Groovy provides a rich set of features for object-oriented programming, making it an excellent choice for developers looking to embrace OOP principles in a clean and expressive syntax. By understanding classes, inheritance, polymorphism, encapsulation, interfaces, and abstract classes, developers can create robust and maintainable applications in Groovy. As you continue to explore Groovy's capabilities, consider how you can leverage OOP to build efficient software solutions that meet the demands of modern programming.

Chapter 4: Building Your First Chatbot with Groovy

They simulate human conversation and can be embedded in websites, mobile apps, and messaging platforms. Groovy, a powerful and flexible programming language that runs on the Java Virtual Machine (JVM), is an excellent choice for building chatbots due to its concise syntax and seamless interoperability with Java libraries.

In this chapter, we will guide you through the process of creating your first chatbot using Groovy. We'll cover the fundamentals of setting up your development environment, structuring your bot's logic, and deploying it for real-world interaction.

4.1 Setting Up Your Development Environment

Before we embark on building our chatbot, we need to ensure that our development environment is configured correctly. Here's a step-by-step guide:

Step 1: Install Groovy

First, you need to install Groovy on your machine. You can download it from the [Groovy official website](https://groovy-lang.org/download.html). Follow the installation instructions provided for your operating system.

Step 2: Install a Text Editor or IDE

Next, you'll want a good text editor or integrated development environment (IDE) to write your Groovy code. Popular choices include:

IntelliJ IDEA: A powerful IDE that supports Groovy

natively.

Eclipse: With the Groovy plugin, Eclipse becomes a solid option.

Visual Studio Code: Lightweight and extensible, with Groovy support through extensions. ### Step 3: Set Up Your Project Structure

Create a new project folder for your chatbot. Inside this folder, set up the following structure:
```

my-chatbot/ src/

main/

groovy/

MyChatbot.groovy build.gradle
```

The `build.gradle` file will be used to manage dependencies and build configurations. ### Step 4: Create a Build Script

Add the following content to your `build.gradle` file to set up Groovy as a dependency:

```groovy
plugins {
id 'groovy'
}
repositories { mavenCentral()
}
dependencies {
implementation 'org.codehaus.groovy:groovy-all:3.0.9'
}
```

With this setup, Gradle will handle dependency management for your Groovy project. ## 4.2 Designing the Chatbot Logic

Now that our environment is ready, let's create a simple chatbot that responds to user input using predefined commands.

Step 1: Writing the Bot Code

Open `MyChatbot.groovy` and add the following code:

```groovy
class MyChatbot {

static void main(String[] args) {

println "Welcome to My Chatbot! Type 'exit' to quit."
String input

Scanner scanner = new Scanner(System.in)

while (true) { print "> "

input = scanner.nextLine()
```

```
if (input.equalsIgnoreCase("exit")) { println "Goodbye!"
break
} else {
String response = generateResponse(input) println
response
}
}
}
static String generateResponse(String userInput) { switch
(userInput.toLowerCase()) {
case "hello":
return "Hello! How can I assist you today?" case "how are
you?":
return "I'm just a bot, but thanks for asking!" case "what is
your name?":
return "I am MyChatbot, your virtual assistant." default:
return "I'm sorry, I didn't understand that. Can you try
something else?"
}
}
}
```
` ` `

Step 2: Breaking Down the Code

Class Definition: We define a class `MyChatbot` that
contains our bot logic.

58

Main Function: The `main` method serves as an entry point. We initialize a `Scanner` to read user input and enter a loop to continuously process that input.

Input Handling: The user can type commands in the console, and the bot responds based on predefined patterns in the `generateResponse` method.

Response Logic: The `generateResponse` method uses a switch statement to provide answers based on common inputs, returning a default message for unrecognized commands.

4.3 Running Your Chatbot

To run your chatbot, navigate to your project directory in the terminal and execute:

```bash
./gradlew run
```

If you're using Windows, the command may vary slightly. This will compile your code and start the chatbot. Test different inputs to see how your chatbot responds.

4.4 Enhancing Your Chatbot

With a basic chatbot operational, you can enhance its capabilities:

Integration with APIs: Introduce external services, such as weather or news APIs, to provide dynamic responses.

Natural Language Processing (NLP): Utilize libraries like OpenNLP or TensorFlow to enhance your bot's understanding of user inputs.

Deployment: Consider deploying your chatbot on platforms like Heroku or AWS to make it accessible to users online.

In this chapter, you learned how to build your first chatbot using Groovy. We covered the essentials from setting up the development environment to writing simple interactive logic. As you grow more comfortable with Groovy, you can delve deeper into advanced features, integrate third-party services, and take your chatbot project to the next level.

Understanding the Chatbot Architecture

This chapter delves into the fundamental components of chatbot architecture, providing insights into how these structures function, the technologies that underpin them, and their practical applications.

1. The Components of Chatbot Architecture

Understanding chatbot architecture requires a breakdown of its primary components. Most chatbots can be divided into the following layers:

1.1 User Interface

The user interface (UI) is the front-end layer where interactions occur. This could be in the form of:

Text-based Interfaces: These include chat windows on websites, messaging apps, or SMS-based systems. Users input their queries or commands in written language.

Voice Interfaces: In voice-enabled chatbots, users interact through speech. These are commonly found in virtual assistants like Amazon's Alexa, Google Assistant, and Apple's Siri.

1.2 Natural Language Processing (NLP)

Natural Language Processing is the core technology that enables a chatbot to understand and interpret human language. Key components of NLP include:

Intent Recognition: This involves identifying the purpose behind the user's input. For example, a user saying "I want to book a flight" indicates an intent to engage in the booking process.

Entity Recognition: This helps in extracting relevant information from the user input. For example, in the sentence "Book a flight to New York for tomorrow," "New York" is the entity, while "tomorrow" provides the necessary date context.

Sentiment Analysis: This component assesses the emotional tone behind the words—whether the user's message conveys positivity, negativity, or neutrality.

1.3 Dialog Management

Dialog management serves as the brain of the chatbot. It is responsible for keeping track of the conversation context, managing flow, and ensuring that interactions are logical and meaningful. Key aspects include:

State Management: Maintaining the state of the conversation, which could involve remembering user preferences or previous questions.

Response Generation: Crafting appropriate responses based on the user input and the dialog context. This can be either rule-based or generated through machine learning algorithms.

1.4 Backend Integration

The backend of a chatbot architecture connects it to necessary databases, APIs, and other external systems. This integration enables the chatbot to fetch real-time information, manage transactions, or perform specific actions like sending data to a user. Key elements include:

Database Connectivity: Storing and retrieving user data, conversation logs, and interactions can provide context for more personalized responses.

API Integration: Chatbots often depend on third-party services for tasks such as payment, ordering, or accessing updated information from external databases.

1.5 Learning and Improvement

As the chatbot interacts with users, it can improve its performance through machine learning. Continuous learning mechanisms allow the chatbot to adapt its responses and understand user preferences better. This involves:

Feedback Loops: Collecting user feedback and ratings can guide the chatbot in adjusting its responses and behavior.

Training Mechanisms: Periodically updating the model with new data ensures that the chatbot remains relevant and effective in its responses.

2. Types of Chatbot Architectures

The architecture of chatbots can vary based on their design and intended purpose. Two primary types of architectures are:

2.1 Rule-Based Chatbots

These chatbots operate based on predefined rules and scripts. They follow a specific pathway guided by conditional statements that dictate responses to user inputs. While rule-based chatbots are simpler and easier to implement, their ability to handle varied interactions is limited. They are most effective for straightforward tasks, such as answering FAQs or basic customer service inquiries.

2.2 AI-Powered Chatbots

Conversely, AI-powered chatbots leverage machine learning, NLP, and advanced algorithms to understand and respond to user inquiries more flexibly. These chatbots can learn from their interactions, making them capable of handling more complex scenarios. They can manage multi-turn conversations and better interpret contextual nuances, which significantly enhances user experience.

3. Development Platforms and Tools

A variety of tools and platforms facilitate the creation of chatbots. Some popular ones include:

Dialogflow: Developed by Google, this platform provides powerful NLP capabilities and integrates with multiple messaging channels.

Microsoft Bot Framework: It offers a comprehensive environment for building and deploying chatbots across various platforms.

Rasa: An open-source framework that allows for building contextual AI assistants without being locked into proprietary platforms.

IBM Watson Assistant: IBM's AI solution excels in enterprise-level chatbot solutions that require advanced features and integration capabilities.

By grasping the foundational components and capabilities of both rule-based and AI-powered chatbots, developers can create more intuitive, efficient, and responsive systems, thereby enriching user interactions and ultimately driving business success. In the following chapters, we will explore specific use cases, design considerations, and best practices to ensure the successful implementation of chatbots in various domains.

Writing a Basic Groovy Chatbot

Groovy, a versatile language that runs on the Java platform, is an excellent choice for developing a chatbot due to its simplicity and ease of integration with existing Java frameworks. In this chapter, we will guide you step-by-step in creating a basic chatbot using Groovy. By the end of this chapter, you will have the foundational knowledge to expand and customize your chatbot for various applications.

Prerequisites

Before delving into the code, ensure you have the following set up:

Java Development Kit (JDK): Groovy runs on the Java

platform, so you'll need the JDK installed on your machine. You can download the latest version from the [Oracle website](https://www.oracle.com/java/technologies/javase-downloads.html) or adopt OpenJDK.

Groovy Installation: Install Groovy by downloading it from the [Groovy website](https://groovy-lang.org/download.html) or using a package manager like SDKMAN.

Development Environment: You can use any text editor you prefer (e.g., Visual Studio Code, IntelliJ IDEA, or Eclipse). Ensure you install any necessary plugins for Groovy support.

Basic Understanding of Groovy: Familiarize yourself with the basic syntax and constructs of Groovy, as this chapter will build upon that knowledge.

Step 1: Setting Up the Project

Create a new directory for your chatbot project. Inside this directory, create a new Groovy file named

`Chatbot.groovy`. We'll implement our chatbot's functionality in this file.

```bash
mkdir GroovyChatbot cd GroovyChatbot touch Chatbot.groovy
```

Step 2: Writing Basic Chat Logic

We'll start by creating a simple command-line chatbot that can respond to a few predefined inputs. Open

`Chatbot.groovy` and add the following code:

```groovy
class Chatbot { def responses = [
"hi": "Hello! How can I help you today?",
"how are you": "I'm just a bunch of code, but I'm doing great!", "bye": "Goodbye! Have a nice day!",
"help": "Sure, I can help you. What do you need?"
]
def getResponse(String input) {
return responses.get(input.toLowerCase(), "Sorry, I didn't understand that.")
}
def chat() {
println "Welcome to Groovy Chatbot! Type 'bye' to exit." while (true) {
print "> "
def userInput = System.console().readLine() if (userInput.toLowerCase() == "bye") {
println "Exiting chat." break
}
println getResponse(userInput)
}
}
}
```

```
new Chatbot().chat()
```
```

### Explanation of the Code

**Class Definition**: We define a `Chatbot` class that contains our chatbot logic.

**Responses Map**: A map of predefined responses (`responses`) is created. The keys represent user input, and the values represent corresponding chatbot responses.

**getResponse Method**: This method takes user input as a parameter, converts it to lowercase for case- insensitive matching, and retrieves the appropriate response from the map. If the input doesn't match any key, a default message is returned.

**chat Method**: This method handles the main interaction loop. It welcomes the user, waits for input, and calls `getResponse` to generate the chatbot's reply until the user types "bye".

## Step 3: Running the Chatbot

To run your chatbot, open your terminal in the project directory and execute the following command:

```bash
groovy Chatbot.groovy
```
```

You should see the welcome message, and you can start chatting with your bot. Type "hi", "how are you", or "help", and observe the responses. To exit, simply type "bye".

Step 4: Extending Your Chatbot

Now that you have a basic chatbot, it's time to think about extending its capabilities. Here are some ideas you could implement:

Natural Language Processing (NLP):

Integrate libraries like Apache OpenNLP or Stanford NLP to parse and understand user input better.

External Data Sources:

Fetch responses from an external API or database to provide dynamic content.

Implement a weather chatbot that uses a weather API to provide real-time information.

User Context:

Maintain a simple state management system to remember previous interactions and provide context-aware responses.

Graphical User Interface (GUI):

Create a GUI for your chatbot using frameworks like JavaFX to enhance user interaction.

Connect to Messaging Platforms:

Expand the chatbot to work inside messaging apps like Slack, Telegram, or Discord using their APIs.

As you explore the possibilities, you'll find that the world of chatbots is rich and rewarding, whether for personal projects, customer service, or entertainment. Keep experimenting, and don't hesitate to dive deeper into Groovy's extensive ecosystem. Happy coding!

Chapter 5: APIs and Messaging Automation Essentials

Furthermore, the rise of messaging technologies has propelled automation into the spotlight, allowing organizations to streamline workflows and enhance efficiency. In this chapter, we'll explore how Groovy, a powerful and flexible scripting language, can be utilized to harness the full potential of APIs and messaging automation.

5.1 Understanding APIs ### 5.1.1 What is an API?

An API is a set of rules and protocols that allows different software applications to communicate with each other. It defines the methods and data formats that applications can use to request and exchange information. APIs can be categorized into several types, including:

Open APIs: Available to developers and third-party applications.

Internal APIs: Used within an organization to communicate between internal systems.

Partner APIs: Given to specific business partners for enhanced collaboration.

Composite APIs: Combine multiple API calls into a single request. ### 5.1.2 The Importance of APIs

APIs are critical for modern application development as they enable:

Interoperability: Connecting disparate systems and technologies.

Scalability: Allowing developers to build applications without having to recreate functionalities.

Innovation: Facilitating the integration of third-party functionalities and services. ## 5.2 Messaging Automation Basics

Messaging technology helps facilitate communication between software systems and often plays a crucial

role in automating workflows. Messaging patterns, such as messaging queues and pub/sub models, ensure that messages are transmitted efficiently and accurately between systems.

5.2.1 Key Messaging Patterns

Point-to-Point: A message is sent from one producer to a single consumer.

Publish/Subscribe: Messages are distributed to multiple subscribers, allowing for decoupled communication.

Message Queues: Messages are stored in queues until they can be processed by consumers, ensuring reliability.

5.2.2 Benefits of Messaging Automation

Decoupled Architecture: Systems can operate independently, reducing dependencies.

Reliability and Resilience: Automated systems can recover from failures without manual intervention.

Asynchronous Processing: Tasks can be processed in the background, improving user experience. ## 5.3 Groovy: The Language of Choice

Groovy, a dynamic language for the Java platform, offers a

syntax that is both concise and expressive. Its flexibility and integration capabilities make it perfect for scripting complex API interactions and messaging automation tasks.

5.3.1 Why Groovy for APIs and Messaging?

Ease of Use: Groovy has a gentle learning curve, making it accessible for developers familiar with Java.

Built-in Support for JSON and XML: These data formats are common in APIs.

Excellent Libraries: Groovy has extensive libraries and frameworks, like Grape and Gradle, that simplify dependency management.

5.4 Building APIs with Groovy ### 5.4.1 Setting Up a Simple API

To illustrate how Groovy can be used to create an API, we'll outline the steps for setting up a simple RESTful API using Spring Boot, a popular framework for building APIs in Java and Groovy.

```groovy
@Grab('org.springframework.boot:spring-boot-starter-web') import org.springframework.boot.SpringApplication

import org.springframework.boot.autoconfigure.SpringBootApplication import org.springframework.web.bind.annotation.*

@SpringBootApplication @RestController

class SimpleApi {

@GetMapping('/greet/{name}')
```

```groovy
String greet(@PathVariable String name) { return "Hello,
$name!"
}
}

SpringApplication.run(SimpleApi)
```

In this example, we created a simple API that greets users by their name. The `@GetMapping` annotation maps HTTP GET requests to the `greet` method.

5.4.2 Consuming APIs with Groovy

Groovy makes it easy to consume APIs via its built-in support for HTTP operations. Here's how you can make a GET request to an external API and parse the JSON response:

```groovy
@Grab('org.codehaus.gpars:gpars:1.2.1')

import groovy.json.JsonSlurper import groovyx.net.http.RESTClient

def client = new RESTClient('https://jsonplaceholder.typicode.com/') def response = client.get(path: 'posts/1')


def post = new JsonSlurper().parseText(response.data.toString()) println "Title: ${post.title}, Body: ${post.body}"
```

In this snippet, `RESTClient` is used to make a GET request to retrieve a post, and `JsonSlurper` is employed to parse the JSON response.

5.5 Messaging Automation with Groovy

5.5.1 Using Groovy with Messaging Systems

Groovy can easily interact with various messaging systems such as RabbitMQ, Kafka, and ActiveMQ. Let's explore a simple example using RabbitMQ to demonstrate messaging automation.

```groovy
@Grab('org.apache.activemq:activemq-spring-boot-starter:2.2.0')

import org.springframework.beans.factory.annotation.Autowired
import org.springframework.jms.annotation.JmsListener

import org.springframework.stereotype.Component

@Component
class MessageListener {

@JmsListener(destination = 'myQueue') void receiveMessage(String message) {

println "Received Message: $message"

}
}
```

In this example, we set up a listener that waits for messages on `myQueue`. When a message is received, it is printed out.

5.5.2 Sending Messages

73

Sending messages to a queue can be done easily in Groovy as follows:

```groovy
@Grab('org.apache.activemq:activemq-spring-boot-starter:2.2.0')

import org.springframework.jms.core.JmsTemplate

import org.springframework.beans.factory.annotation.Autowired
import org.springframework.stereotype.Component

@Component

class MessageSender {

@Autowired

JmsTemplate jmsTemplate

void sendMessage(String message) { jmsTemplate.convertAndSend('myQueue', message) println "Sent Message: $message"

}

}
```

Here, we defined the `MessageSender` class, which takes a message and sends it to `myQueue`.

In this chapter, we explored the essentials of APIs and messaging automation, emphasizing the capabilities of Groovy as a powerful tool for developers. By understanding how to create and consume APIs, alongside automating messaging workflows, you'll be equipped to build flexible and scalable applications.

APIs, and How Do Chatbots Use Them

An API serves as a set of rules and protocols that dictate how software applications interact with one another. By allowing disparate systems to exchange data and functionality, APIs help foster innovation and enhance user experiences across a myriad of applications, including chatbots.

Chatbots, powered by artificial intelligence, are designed to simulate human conversation and provide valuable responses to user queries. While these intelligent systems possess their own capabilities, their effectiveness often hinges on the APIs they leverage. This chapter delves into the nature of APIs, their function in chatbot development, and the benefits they provide to both developers and end-users.

Understanding APIs

At their core, APIs act as intermediaries that allow different software applications to communicate with each other. They expose certain functionality from one system to be utilized by another, making it easier for developers to integrate various services without needing to understand the underlying code.

APIs are typically categorized into three main types:

Open APIs (Public APIs): These are available to developers and third parties, allowing them to build applications that can interact with a service. Examples include the Twitter API, which lets users fetch tweets and post updates, and the Google Maps API, which provides mapping functionalities.

Internal APIs (Private APIs): These are used within an organization and are not exposed to external developers. Internal APIs can streamline processes, improve resource sharing among different departments, and enhance the overall productivity of a business.

Composite APIs: These allow developers to access multiple endpoints in a single call. This can be especially useful when a user needs information from several sources at once, simplifying the requests and reducing latency.

Chatbots: The Interface of Human and Machine

Chatbots utilize natural language processing (NLP) and machine learning to understand user inputs and respond appropriately. Their primary objective is to mimic human conversation and provide satisfactory answers or solutions to inquiries. However, to achieve a high level of intelligence and accuracy, chatbots often require real-time data and functionality that may reside outside their core programming. This is where APIs come into play.

How Chatbots Use APIs

Chatbots leverage APIs to extend their capabilities, access external information, and interact with various services. Here are some key ways APIs are integrated within chatbot design:

1. Information Retrieval

One primary function of chatbots is to deliver information in response to user queries. For instance, a customer service chatbot for an airline may need to access flight schedules, ticket prices, and booking statuses. By utilizing the carrier's API, the chatbot can retrieve real-time data, ensuring users receive accurate and up-to-date information.

2. Performing Actions on Behalf of Users

Many chatbots are designed to facilitate actions for users, such as booking appointments, ordering products, or making reservations. To accomplish this, chatbots rely on APIs to perform actions in the background. For example, a food delivery chatbot may utilize a restaurant's API to place an order and process payment.

3. Integrating with Other Services

To enhance user experiences, chatbots can integrate with various third-party services using APIs. For instance, a chatbot used in e-commerce can connect with payment gateways, inventory management systems, and shipping services. This seamless integration allows users to complete transactions without navigating away from the chat interface.

4. Personalization

Utilizing APIs, chatbots can access user data stored in databases or external systems. This data enables chatbots to deliver personalized responses based on the user's preferences and history. For instance, a chatbot in a retail environment might retrieve a user's previous purchases to suggest relevant products.

5. Collecting Feedback and Learning

APIs can also assist chatbots in gathering feedback from users. By integrating with survey or feedback collection platforms, chatbots can analyze user sentiment and make adjustments to improve interactions. Moreover, data gathered can be fed back into machine learning algorithms to enhance the chatbot's performance over time.

The Benefits of APIs for Chatbots

APIs confer numerous advantages to chatbot development, including:

Efficiency: Developers can utilize existing APIs rather than building intricate systems from scratch, accelerating the development process and reducing costs.

Scalability: API-driven chatbots can easily scale their capabilities by integrating new services as needed, allowing businesses to adapt to changing requirements.

Enhanced Features: APIs provide access to advanced functionalities, such as NLP and machine learning algorithms, enabling chatbots to deliver more sophisticated interactions.

Data Access: APIs facilitate real-time data access, making chatbots capable of retrieving and processing information quickly in response to user inquiries.

APIs are the backbone of modern chatbot functionality. By enabling chatbots to communicate with various systems, access real-time data, and perform actions on behalf of users, APIs ensure that these digital assistants are more than mere automated responders. They allow chatbots to deliver personalized, efficient, and user-friendly interactions that cater to a multitude of needs.

Automating Responses with Groovy and Webhooks

In this chapter, we will explore how to harness the power of Groovy—a dynamic language for the Java platform—alongside webhooks to streamline and automate responses in various applications.

1. Understanding Webhooks

Webhooks are user-defined HTTP callbacks that are triggered by specific events in web applications. When an event occurs, a server makes an HTTP request to a predefined URL, which can then execute a command or trigger actions within your application. This pattern allows for real-time data transfer and communication between systems.

1.1 Real-world Scenarios

Consider the following scenarios where webhooks can be useful:

Payment Processing: When a user completes a payment, a webhook can notify your application to update order status to 'Paid' and send confirmation emails.

GitHub Events: On every push to a GitHub repository, a webhook can trigger deployment scripts to automatically deliver updates to production environments.

Customer Feedback: A webhook can send user feedback captured through a form directly to your application, removing the need for manual intervention.

2. The Role of Groovy in Automation

Groovy enhances Java's capabilities with a more intuitive and flexible syntax, making it particularly suitable for scripting and rapid development. It integrates seamlessly with Java libraries and frameworks, providing access to powerful APIs while maintaining simplicity.

2.1 Key Groovy Features

Dynamic Typing: Groovy's dynamic typing can speed up development time, as you do not need to explicitly declare data types.

Closures: Groovy's closures allow for the creation of anonymous functions, enabling you to define operations to be performed later.

Easy Integration: Groovy integrates easily with existing Java structures, making it a great fit for legacy systems that require modern customizations.

3. Setting Up Your Environment

To get started, you'll need a few components:

A Groovy Development Environment: You can use tools like IntelliJ IDEA or Groovy Console for coding.

A Web Server: Set up a local or cloud-based server capable of receiving HTTP requests. Tools like Express.js or Spring Boot can be used to handle incoming webhook calls.

A Testing Tool: Postman or similar tools for testing webhook functionality. ### 3.1 Installing Groovy

Download and install Groovy from the official website.

Set up environment variables to use Groovy from the command line.

Verify the installation by running `groovy -version`. ## 4. Creating a Simple Webhook Listener in Groovy

Now, let's create a simple server that listens for incoming webhooks. We will be using the `Ratpack` framework, a set of Groovy-based tools for building web applications.

4.1 Sample Code

```groovy
import ratpack.server.RatpackServer

RatpackServer.start { server -> server.handlers { chain ->

chain.get("webhook") { ctx ->

def payload = ctx.getRequest().getBody().getText() println "Received webhook with payload: ${payload}"


// Here, you can process the payload as per your application's requirement
ctx.getResponse().status(200).send("Webhook received")
}
}
}
```

4.2 Running the Server To run the server:

Save the above code in a file named `WebhookListener.groovy`.

Execute the script with the command `groovy WebhookListener.groovy`.

Your server will be running on

`http://localhost:5050/webhook`, ready to accept requests! ## 5. Sending Test Webhook Events

Once your server is running, you can test it using a tool like Postman:

Set the request type to POST and the URL to `http://localhost:5050/webhook`.

In the body, select "raw" and choose JSON; then input your test payload:

```json
{
"event": "order_created", "data": {
"orderId": "1234",
"amount": 150.99
}
}
```

Click Send. You should see the printed message in your console, confirming the reception of the webhook.

6. Automating Responses Based on Webhook Events

Now that we can receive webhooks, let's automate some responses. Depending on the event type, we'll take different actions:

6.1 Using Conditions

Modify the webhook handling logic to process events based on types:

```groovy
chain.post("webhook") { ctx ->
def payload = ctx.getRequest().getBody().getText()
def json = new groovy.json.JsonSlurper().parseText(payload)

switch (json.event) { case "order_created":
sendOrderConfirmation(json.data.orderId,
json.data.amount)
ctx.getResponse().status(200).send("Order  confirmation
sent.") break
// Handle other events... default:
ctx.getResponse().status(400).send("Event           not
recognized.")
}
}

void  sendOrderConfirmation(String   orderId,  double
amount) {
// Logic to send email or notification
println "Sending confirmation for Order ID: $orderId,
Amount: $amount"
}
```

In this chapter, we explored the seamless automation of responses using Groovy and webhooks. By integrating these technologies, developers can significantly enhance communication capabilities in their applications. As you continue to develop your automated systems, remember the principles of modularity and maintainability—keeping your code organized will facilitate future adjustments.

Chapter 6: Integrating Chatbots with Slack

In this chapter, we focus on how to integrate chatbots with Slack using Groovy, a dynamic language built on the Java platform.

We will explore the Slack API, set up a basic Slack application, and develop a simple chatbot that interacts with users in real-time. By the end of this chapter, you will be equipped to implement chatbots in your own Slack workspace, helping your team optimize communication and productivity.

6.1 Understanding Slack and Its API

Slack is a messaging platform designed for teamwork, allowing users to communicate through channels, direct messages, and integrations with other apps. To create a chatbot in Slack, we must first familiarize ourselves with the Slack API. The API provides several methods to interact with Slack's features, including sending messages, receiving events, managing channels, and more.

6.1.1 Registering Your Slack App

Create a Slack Account: If you haven't already, register for a Slack account and create a new workspace.

Visit the Slack API Website: Go to [Slack API](https://api.slack.com/apps) and click on "Create New App."

Configure Your App: Fill in the necessary information, such as the app name and the workspace where it will be used. Once created, you can configure the app's settings.

6.1.2 Enabling Permissions

Before your chatbot can start functioning, you need to set the appropriate permissions:

Add Bot User: Under the "Features" section, select "Bot Users" and click "Add a Bot User." This bot represents your chatbot in Slack.

Set Scopes: Navigate to the "OAuth & Permissions" section and add scopes relevant to your bot's functionality. For example, `chat:write` allows the bot to send messages.

After configuring permissions, install the app to your workspace, which will generate an OAuth token necessary for authenticating API requests.

6.2 Setting Up the Groovy Environment

To create our Slack chatbot in Groovy, we need to set up a suitable environment. ### 6.2.1 Installing Groovy

Download and Install: Visit [Groovy's official website](https://groovy-lang.org/download.html) and follow the installation instructions for your operating system.

Set Up Your Development Environment: You can use any IDE that supports Groovy, such as IntelliJ IDEA or Eclipse with the Groovy plugin.

6.2.2 Adding Dependencies

To interact with Slack's API, we will use the HTTPBuilder library to simplify HTTP requests. You can add dependencies using Grape or the Gradle build tool.

Example using Grape:

```groovy
@Grab(group='org.codehaus.gpars', module='gpars', version='1.2.1')
@Grab(group='org.codehaus.groovy.modules.http-builder', module='http-builder', version='0.7.1') import groovyx.net.http.RESTClient
```

6.3 Developing the Chatbot

Now that our environment is set up, let's develop a simple chatbot that responds to user messages in Slack. ### 6.3.1 The Bot's Logic

We'll create a basic bot that listens to messages in a specific channel and responds with a greeting when a user mentions it.

```groovy
import groovyx.net.http.RESTClient

import static groovyx.net.http.ContentType.JSON

def token = 'YOUR_SLACK_BOT_TOKEN'

def slackClient = new RESTClient('https://slack.com/api/')

def receiveMessage() {

def response = slackClient.post( path: 'chat.postMessage',
```

```groovy
query: [token: token, channel: 'CHANNEL_ID', text:
'Hello! How can I assist you today?'], requestContentType:
JSON
)

if (response.data.ok) {

println "Message sent: ${response.data.ts}"

} else {

println "Error sending message: ${response.data.error}"

}

}

receiveMessage()
```

6.3.2 Responding to User Input

To make our bot interactive, we can extend its capabilities to respond dynamically based on user input. Here's how you can capture messages and formulate responses:

```groovy
def handleUserMessage(message) {

if (message.contains("@your_bot_name")) {

return "Hello! I'm here to help. What do you need
assistance with?"

}

return "I'm not sure how to respond to that.";

}
```

```
```

By parsing incoming messages and checking for mentions of the bot, we can provide contextual responses. ## 6.4 Hosting Your Bot

To make your chatbot operational, it needs to be hosted so that it can interact with users in real-time. You can choose various options such as a cloud service (AWS, Heroku) or your local server.

6.4.1 Setting Up a Web Server

You can set up a simple web server using Groovy to listen for incoming messages:

```groovy
@Grab('org.eclipse.jetty:jetty-server:9.4.31.v20200723')
import org.eclipse.jetty.server.Server

import org.eclipse.jetty.servlet.ServletContextHandler
import org.eclipse.jetty.servlet.ServletHolder

def server = new Server(8080)

def context = new ServletContextHandler(ServletContextHandler.SESSIONS) context.contextPath = "/"

server.handler = context

context.addServlet(new ServletHolder(new SlackEventServlet()), "/slack/events") server.start()

server.join()
```

This setup listens for incoming Slack events, allowing your bot to respond appropriately.

Integrating chatbots with Slack using Groovy represents an exciting opportunity for enhancing team communication. In this chapter, you learned about the Slack API, how to set up a Groovy environment, and how to create an interactive chatbot. As businesses increasingly turn to automation and AI solutions, your ability to develop such integrations will be a valuable skill..

Building a Slack Bot with Groovy

This chapter aims to guide you through the process of creating a simple yet effective Slack bot using Groovy, a powerful and expressive programming language for the Java platform. By the end of this chapter, you will have your very own Slack bot that can respond to messages and perform basic commands!

What You'll Need

Before we dive into the coding, ensure you have the following prerequisites:

JDK (Java Development Kit): Ensure you have the latest version installed on your machine.

Groovy: Install the latest version of Groovy. You can download it from the [Groovy website](https://groovy-lang.org/download.html).

Slack Account: A Slack workspace where you can create and test your bot.

Slack App Credentials: You will need to create a new Slack app to obtain the app token and signing secret.

Step 1: Creating a Slack App

Go to Slack API: Navigate to [Slack API](https://api.slack.com/apps).

Create a New App: Click on "Create New App," choose a name for your bot, and select your workspace.

Bot User: In the OAuth & Permissions section, add a Bot User. Set its display name and default username.

Scopes: Add the necessary OAuth scopes for your bot. For basic functionality, you can add:

`chat:write`: To send messages.

`chat:read`: To read messages.

Install App: Once you have configured the required permissions, install the app to your workspace. You will obtain a "Bot User OAuth Token," which you will use in your code.

Step 2: Setting Up Your Groovy Environment

To get started, you can create a new directory for your Slack bot project. Inside the directory, create the following file structure:

```
/slackbot src

SlackBot.groovy
```

Now, let's write the code in `SlackBot.groovy`. ### Step 3: Coding the Slack Bot

Open up `SlackBot.groovy` and begin by importing necessary libraries:

91

```groovy
@Grab(group='org.codehaus.gpars', module='gpars',
version='1.2.1')    @Grab(group='com.squareup.okhttp3',
module='okhttp', version='3.12.0')


import          groovy.json.JsonSlurper          import
groovy.json.JsonBuilder import okhttp3.*
import java.util.concurrent.TimeUnit
```

Next, define the main class and some constants:

```groovy
class SlackBot {

static final String SLACK_TOKEN = 'xoxb-your-bot-user-
oauth-token' static final String SLACK_API_URL =
'https://slack.com/api/'

static final String CHANNEL_ID = 'your-channel-id'

def client = new OkHttpClient.Builder()

.connectTimeout(10, TimeUnit.SECONDS)

.readTimeout(10, TimeUnit.SECONDS)

.build()

// Main method

static void main(String[] args) { new SlackBot().run()

}

void run() {

sendMessageToSlack("Hello from Groovy Slack Bot!")
```

```groovy
// Example of using your bot to listen to messages
listenForMessages()
}
}
```

Here, replace `xoxb-your-bot-user-oauth-token` with your actual bot token and `your-channel-id` with the channel ID you want your bot to post messages in.

Step 4: Sending Messages to Slack

Now, let's implement the method to send messages:

```groovy
void sendMessageToSlack(String message) { def json =
new JsonBuilder()

json {

channel CHANNEL_ID text message

}

RequestBody                    body                    =
RequestBody.create(MediaType.parse("application/json;
charset=utf-8"), json.toString())

Request request = new Request.Builder()

.url(SLACK_API_URL + 'chat.postMessage')

.post(body)

.addHeader('Authorization', "Bearer $SLACK_TOKEN")

.build()

client.newCall(request).enqueue(new Callback() { void
```

```groovy
onFailure(Call call, IOException e) {
println("Failed to send message: ${e.message}")
}
void onResponse(Call call, Response response) throws
IOException { if (!response.isSuccessful()) {
println("Error: ${response.message()}")
} else {
println("Message sent successfully!")
}
}
})
}
```

Step 5: Listening for Messages

For a real bot experience, you will want your bot to listen
for incoming messages. Slack uses events to notify your
bot about happenings in channels. To set this up, you will
need to implement a simple HTTP server to listen for
event calls from Slack.

Add this to your `SlackBot.groovy` file:

```groovy
void listenForMessages() { def http = new HttpServer()
http.start(8080)
println("Listening for events on port 8080")
http.addListener(new HttpListener() {
```

94

```groovy
void onRequest(HttpRequest request, HttpResponse
response) { def payload = new
JsonSlurper().parseText(request.body)

if ('event_callback' == payload.type) { def event =
payload.event

if (event.type == 'message' && event.channel ==
CHANNEL_ID) { String user = event.user ?: "someone"

String text = event.text

println("Message from ${user}: ${text}")

}

}


response.status = 200 response.send('OK')

}

})

}

}
```
```

### Step 6: Running Your Bot

With your code set up, you can now run your bot:

Open a terminal and navigate to your project directory.

Run the bot using the Groovy command:

```bash

groovy src/SlackBot.groovy

```
` ` `
```

Conclusion

Congratulations! You have built your first Slack bot using Groovy. This bot can send messages to your Slack workspace and listen to incoming messages in real-time. You can extend its capabilities by adding more features, such as responding to specific commands, integrating with external APIs, or processing data.

Now that you have a basic understanding of building a Slack bot, consider exploring advanced topics such as:

Creating interactive components (buttons, dialogs) using Slack's Block Kit.

Storing user data in a database for more personalized responses.

Deploying your bot using cloud services to keep it running 24/7.

Managing Slack Events and Commands

This chapter will guide you on how to effectively manage Slack events and commands using Groovy. ## 1. Introduction to Slack Events and Commands

Before diving into the implementation, it's crucial to understand what Slack events and commands are. ### 1.1 Slack Events

Slack events are real-time notifications that are sent to

your application when specific actions occur in Slack. These can range from user interactions (like messages being posted) to changes in workspace settings.

Events are a core part of building interactive integrations with Slack. ### 1.2 Slack Commands

Commands provide an interface for users to interact with your application directly from Slack. A command typically starts with a forward slash (e.g., `/weather`). When a user inputs a command, Slack sends an HTTP request to your server, which you must handle appropriately.

2. Setting Up Your Groovy Environment

To get started with managing Slack events and commands in Groovy, you'll need to set up your environment.

2.1 Install Groovy

You can download and install Groovy from the [official website](http://groovy-lang.org/download.html). You might also consider using a build tool like Gradle for dependency management.

2.2 Create a Slack App

Go to the [Slack API](https://api.slack.com/apps) page and create a new app.

Configure the app's permissions and settings to enable events and commands.

Note your "Signing Secret" and "OAuth Token," which will be crucial for authenticating your requests. ## 3. Implementing a Basic Slack Event Listener

This section will demonstrate how to create a simple Slack event listener using Groovy. ### 3.1 Dependencies

If you're using Gradle, you'll want to add the following dependencies to your `build.gradle` file:

```groovy
dependencies {

implementation            'org.codehaus.groovy:groovy:3.0.9'
implementation 'org.slf4j:slf4j-api:1.7.30'

implementation    'org.slf4j:slf4j-simple:1.7.30'    //    for
logging

}
```

3.2 Create a Service to Handle Events

Create a Groovy class, `SlackEventService`, to handle incoming events:

```groovy
import groovy.json.JsonSlurper import spark.Spark

class SlackEventService {

private    static    final    String    SIGNING_SECRET    =
'YOUR_SLACK_SIGNING_SECRET'

static void main(String[] args) { Spark.port(3000)

Spark.post('/slack/events',        {       req,       res       ->
handleEvent(req.body())

})

}

static void handleEvent(String body) {

def json = new JsonSlurper().parseText(body) if (json.type
== 'url_verification') {
```

```groovy
    return json.challenge
}


// Handle message events
if (json.type == 'event_callback') { def event = json.event
println "Received event: ${event.type}"
if (event.type == 'message' && !event.subtype) {
respondToMessage(event)
}
}
}

static void respondToMessage(def event) {
// Your logic to respond to messages
println "Responding to message from user ${event.user}: ${event.text}"
// Here, you can send a response back to Slack using the chat.postMessage API
}
}
```

3.3 Running the Application

Run your application using the `groovy` command. Make sure that your application is accessible from the internet (consider using services like ngrok for testing). Update your Slack app's Event Subscriptions with the URL where your app is hosted.

4. Handling Slack Commands

4.1 Implementing a Command Handler

To manage Slack commands, you can expand on your existing service:

```groovy
Spark.post('/slack/commands',    {    req,    res    ->
handleCommand(req.body())
})
static void handleCommand(String body) {
def params = body.split("&").collectEntries { param -> def
parts = param.split("=")
[(parts[0]): URLDecoder.decode(parts[1], 'UTF-8')]
}
// Process the command
if    (params['command']    ==    '/your_command')    {
sendResponse(params['response_url'],    "This    is    your
command response!")
}
}
static void sendResponse(String responseUrl, String text)
{ def httpClient = new HttpClient()
def response = httpClient.post(responseUrl, [ 'text': text,
'response_type': 'in_channel'
```

```
])
println "Response sent with status ${response.status}"
}
```
` ` `

4.2 Use Cases for Commands

Commands can be used to trigger various functionalities, such as querying a database, retrieving user information, or interacting with other APIs. The above example demonstrates a basic implementation, but the flexibility allows for more complex interactions.

5. Testing and Debugging

When developing Slack integrations, testing and debugging is crucial.

Logging: Use SLF4J or another logging framework to capture important information and debug issues.

Postman: Use Postman or a similar tool to simulate requests to your endpoints to ensure they are working as expected.

Slack's Event Subscription Testing: Use the Slack interface to simulate events and check how your application responds.

Managing Slack events and commands in Groovy allows you to build interactive applications that enhance collaboration within teams. By following the steps and examples outlined in this chapter, you can create a foundational setup that you can further expand according to your application's requirements. As you advance, consider exploring more complex interactions, like threading messages or managing conversation histories.

Chapter 7: Creating Bots for Discord

In this chapter, we will explore how to create a Discord bot using Groovy—a powerful scripting language that runs on the Java platform. We will cover the essentials, from setting up your development environment to deploying your bot.

7.1 Setting Up Your Environment

Before we dive into coding, we need to prepare our environment to develop a Discord bot: ### 7.1.1 Install Java Development Kit (JDK)

Ensure that you have the latest version of the JDK installed on your machine. Groovy runs on the Java Virtual Machine (JVM), and having the JDK is essential for the development process.

Download the JDK from the [Oracle website](https://www.oracle.com/java/technologies/java se-jdk11- downloads.html) or your package manager if you are using Linux.

Follow the installation instructions specific to your operating system. ### 7.1.2 Install Groovy

Next, install Groovy. You can download it from the [Groovy website](https://groovy-lang.org/download.html) or use a package manager.

Using SDKMAN (recommended):

```
```

curl -s https://get.sdkman.io | bash

source "$HOME/.sdkman/bin/sdkman-init.sh" sdk install groovy

```
```

7.1.3 Set Up Your Editor

Choose a text editor or IDE that supports Groovy. Some popular options include:

IntelliJ IDEA (with Groovy plugin)

Eclipse (with Groovy plugin)

Visual Studio Code (with Groovy extension) ### 7.1.4 Create a New Project

Create a new project directory for your bot and navigate into it:

```bash
mkdir DiscordBot cd DiscordBot
```

7.2 Creating a Discord Application

Before writing any code, you'll need to create a Discord application:

Visit the [Discord Developer Portal](https://discord.com/developers/applications).

Click on the "New Application" button.

Name your application and confirm.

Go to the "Bot" tab and click "Add Bot" to create a bot user.

Save your bot token, as you'll need this later in your code. ### 7.2.1 Setting Permissions

In the bot settings, set the necessary permissions your bot will require. If you intend for your bot to manage messages, generate invites, or execute commands, ensure those permissions are granted.

7.2.2 Inviting Your Bot to a Server To test your bot, invite it to a server:

Navigate to the OAuth2 tab.

Under "Scopes," select "bot."

Under "Bot Permissions," select the permissions you granted earlier.

Copy the generated URL and paste it into your web browser to invite the bot to your server. ## 7.3 Coding the Bot

Now it's time to write some Groovy code to create your Discord bot. ### 7.3.1 Adding Dependencies

Our bot will use the JDA (Java Discord API) library. Add the following dependency in your `build.gradle` file:

```groovy
dependencies {
implementation 'net.dv8tion:JDA:4.2.0_227'
}
```

7.3.2 Basic Bot Structure

Create a file named `DiscordBot.groovy` in your project folder:

```groovy
@Grab(group='net.dv8tion',                module='JDA',
```

```
version='4.2.0_227')                                    import net.dv8tion.jda.api.JDABuilder

import net.dv8tion.jda.api.events.message.MessageReceivedEvent import net.dv8tion.jda.api.hooks.ListenerAdapter

class MyBot extends ListenerAdapter { static void main(String[] args) {

String token = "YOUR_BOT_TOKEN"

JDABuilder builder = JDABuilder.createDefault(token) builder.addEventListeners(new MyBot()) builder.build()

}

@Override

void onMessageReceived(MessageReceivedEvent event) { if (event.author.isBot()) {

return

}

if (event.message.contentRaw.equalsIgnoreCase('!hello')) {                    event.channel.sendMessage('Hello, ${event.author.name}!').queue()

}

}

}
```
` ` `

7.3.3 Running Your Bot

To run your bot, simply execute the following command in your terminal:

```bash
groovy DiscordBot.groovy
```

If everything is set up correctly, your bot should come online, and you can test it in your Discord server. Type `!hello` in a channel, and your bot should respond with a friendly message.

7.4 Expanding Your Bot's Functionality

Creating a basic bot is just the beginning. You can expand your bot's functionality by adding features like:

Command Handling: Using a command framework to manage and organize commands more effectively.

Database Integration: Storing data for persistent state across bot sessions using file storage or database connections (e.g., SQLite, MongoDB).

Interactive Commands: Creating commands that respond to user input or integrate with external APIs (like fetching random quotes or weather data).

Example: Weather Command

Here's a small example showing how to integrate an external API to provide weather information based on user input:

```groovy
import groovy.json.JsonSlurper

@Override
```

```
void onMessageReceived(MessageReceivedEvent event) {
if (event.author.isBot()) {

return

}

if (event.message.contentRaw.startsWith('!weather ')) {
def city = event.message.contentRaw.split(' ')[1]

def    weatherData    =    fetchWeatherData(city)
event.channel.sendMessage(weatherData).queue()

}


}

def fetchWeatherData(String city) { def apiKey =
'YOUR_API_KEY'

def                url                =
"http://api.openweathermap.org/data/2.5/weather?q=${
city}&appid=${apiKey}&units=metric" def jsonSlurper =
new JsonSlurper()

def response = jsonSlurper.parse(url.toURL())

return    "The    weather    in    ${response.name}    is
${response.main.temp}°C with

${response.weather[0].description}."

}
```
\ \ \

7.5 Deploying Your Bot

Once your bot is ready and you've tested it in your server,
consider deploying it:

Cloud Solutions: Use services like Heroku, AWS Lambda, or DigitalOcean for hosting.

Docker: Containerizing your bot using Docker can make deployment simpler across various environments.

In this chapter, we covered the process of creating a Discord bot using Groovy. From setting up your development environment to deploying your bot, you now have a solid foundation to build upon. As you expand your skills, consider looking into more advanced features and integrations that can make your bot even more engaging and useful. Discord bots are limited only by your imagination, so get creative and have fun!

Using Groovy to Develop Discord Bots

While languages such as JavaScript and Python dominate the bot development scene, Groovy offers a powerful and concise alternative worth exploring. In this chapter, we will dive into the world of Groovy and how you can harness its capabilities to build effective Discord bots.

What is Groovy?

Groovy is an agile, dynamic language for the Java Virtual Machine (JVM) that enjoys seamless integration with Java. Its syntax is concise and expressive, making it easier for developers to write and maintain code. Groovy is particularly appealing for those already familiar with Java, as it introduces features such as closures, native syntax for lists and maps, and string interpolation, while still retaining interoperability with Java libraries.

Setting Up the Environment

Before we start coding, you need to set up your development environment. Follow these steps to get started:

Install Java Development Kit (JDK): Groovy runs on the JVM, which requires you to have JDK installed. Download it from the [Oracle website](https://www.oracle.com/java/technologies/java se-jdk11- downloads.html) or use an open-source alternative like OpenJDK.

Install Groovy: Download and install Groovy from the official website [groovy- lang.org](https://groovy-lang.org/download.html). You can also use SDKMAN for a more flexible way to manage multiple versions of Groovy.

Set Up a Discord Bot Account:

Go to the [Discord Developer Portal](https://discord.com/developers/applications).

Create a new application and give it a name.

Under the "Bot" tab, click "Add Bot" to generate a bot user.

Copy the bot token, as you'll need it later for authentication.

Invite Your Bot: Generate an OAuth2 URL and select the `bot` scope. Make sure to select the necessary permissions, then use the URL to invite your bot to your server.

Building a Simple Discord Bot in Groovy

Now that your environment is set up, it's time to create a

simple Discord bot using Groovy. For this, we will utilize the popular Java library [JDA (Java Discord API)](https://github.com/DV8FromTheWorld/JDA), which allows us to interact with Discord's API easily.

Step 1: Create a New Groovy Project

You can create a new directory for your bot project. Inside that directory, create a subfolder called `lib` for the dependencies.

Step 2: Add Dependencies

Download the JDA library and any other dependencies (like JSON processing libraries). For Gradle users, you can create a `build.gradle` file with the following content:

```groovy
plugins {

id 'groovy'

}

repositories { mavenCentral()

}

dependencies {

implementation 'net.dv8tion:JDA:5.0.0-alpha.7' // Update to the latest version implementation 'org.codehaus.groovy:groovy:3.0.9' // Or your specific version

}
```

Step 3: Write Your Bot Code

Create a Groovy file named `MyDiscordBot.groovy` in the

project's root directory. Here's a simple bot that responds with "Hello!" when someone sends a message in the server.

```groovy
@Grab(group='net.dv8tion',                module='JDA',
version='5.0.0-alpha.7')

import net.dv8tion.jda.api.JDABuilder

import
net.dv8tion.jda.api.events.message.MessageReceivedEvent import net.dv8tion.jda.api.hooks.ListenerAdapter

class MyDiscordBot extends ListenerAdapter { @Override

void onMessageReceived(MessageReceivedEvent event) {

// Ignore messages from bots if (event.author.isBot()) {

return

}

if (event.message.contentRaw.equalsIgnoreCase('!hello'))
{ event.channel.sendMessage("Hello!").queue()

}

}

}

def main(String[] args) {

def token = "YOUR_BOT_TOKEN_HERE" // Use your
bot's     token     JDABuilder     builder     =
JDABuilder.createDefault(token)
builder.addEventListeners(new MyDiscordBot())

builder.build()
```

```
}
main(args)
```

Step 4: Run Your Bot

You can run your bot from the command line using:

```bash
groovy MyDiscordBot.groovy
```

Once it's running, head over to your Discord server where you invited your bot and type `!hello`. The bot should respond with "Hello!".

Expanding Functionality

The example we've covered is quite basic, but Groovy's expressive syntax allows you to easily expand your bot's functionality. Here are some ideas to enhance your bot:

Command Handling: Implement a command handler to organize multiple commands efficiently rather than putting all logic inside `onMessageReceived`.

Persistent Data: Incorporate a database or flat file storage to remember user preferences.

Interaction with APIs: Utilize various APIs, such as weather or news APIs, to fetch real-time information and bring it into your Discord channel.

Embed Messages: Make use of rich embed features that Discord supports to create visually appealing messages and notifications.

Error Handling: Implement error handling to gracefully manage unexpected situations and user inputs.

Creating Discord bots with Groovy is not only feasible but also enjoyable. With its elegant syntax and Java compatibility, Groovy can speed up your development process while ensuring that your bot remains efficient and easy to maintain. This chapter has provided you with the foundational steps to start your journey in bot development. With your bot up and running, you can now explore the vast array of features offered by the Discord API and unleash your creativity. Happy coding!

Enhancing User Interactions with Discord APIs

With a significant user base, the demand for interactive bots within Discord servers has soared. Groovy, a dynamic language for the Java platform, provides a flexible and productive means to develop Discord bots. This chapter aims to explore how to enhance user interactions using the Discord APIs in Groovy, focusing on the creation of engaging and interactive bots.

Understanding Discord and Its API

Discord provides a rich API that allows developers to interact with its extensive features. The Discord API comprises various endpoints that enable the creation of bots capable of sending messages, embedding rich content, managing interactions, and handling events. The Discord API communicates via HTTP requests and uses

WebSockets to maintain real-time interactions.

Groovy, with its concise syntax and seamless interoperability with Java, makes it an ideal choice for developing Discord bots. Libraries like JDA (Java Discord API) allow developers to harness the functionality of Discord's API while coding in a user-friendly manner.

Setting Up Your Groovy Environment

To get started, ensure you have the following prerequisites:

Java Development Kit (JDK): Install the latest version of JDK.

Groovy: Download and install Groovy, preferably using SDKMAN for easy installation and management.

Maven/Gradle: These are dependency management tools commonly used with Java libraries. #### Creating a Basic Bot

Begin by creating a new Groovy project. If using Maven, your `pom.xml` will need to include the JDA dependency:

```xml
<dependency>
<groupId>net.dv8tion</groupId>
<artifactId>JDA</artifactId>
<version>5.0.0-alpha.8</version>
</dependency>
```

Alternatively, if you're using Gradle, add the following to

your `build.gradle`:

```groovy
dependencies {
implementation 'net.dv8tion:JDA:5.0.0-alpha.8'
}
```

Create a simple bot using the following code structure:

```groovy
import net.dv8tion.jda.api.JDABuilder
import net.dv8tion.jda.api.events.message.MessageReceivedEvent
import net.dv8tion.jda.api.hooks.ListenerAdapter
import javax.security.auth.login.LoginException

class DiscordBot extends ListenerAdapter { @Override
void onMessageReceived(MessageReceivedEvent event) {
if (event.author.isBot()) return

if (event.message.contentRaw.equalsIgnoreCase("!hello"))
{ event.channel.sendMessage("Hello! How can I assist you
today?").queue()
}
}
static void main(String[] args) {
String token = "YOUR_DISCORD_BOT_TOKEN"

try {
```

```groovy
JDABuilder builder = JDABuilder.createDefault(token)
builder.addEventListeners(new                DiscordBot())
builder.build()
} catch (LoginException e) { e.printStackTrace()
}
}
}
```
```

This basic structure sets up an event listener that responds with a friendly greeting when a user types `!hello`. ## Enhancing User Interactions

### Implementing Command Handlers

To enrich user interactions, implementing a command handler is crucial. This modularizes your code and allows for cleaner management of multiple commands.

Here's an example of a simple command handler:

```groovy
class CommandHandler {

Map<String, Closure> commands = [:]

void registerCommand(String cmd, Closure action) {
commands.put(cmd.toLowerCase(), action)
}

void          executeCommand(String          cmd,
MessageReceivedEvent              event)              {
commands.get(cmd.toLowerCase())?.call(event)
}
```
```

```
}
```

Now, in your `onMessageReceived` method, use this command handler:

```groovy
CommandHandler commandHandler = new CommandHandler()

commandHandler.registerCommand("hello", { event ->
event.channel.sendMessage("Hello! How can I assist you today?").queue()
})

commandHandler.registerCommand("help", { event ->
event.channel.sendMessage("Available commands: !hello, !help").queue()
})

@Override
void onMessageReceived(MessageReceivedEvent event) {
if (event.author.isBot()) return

String content = event.message.contentRaw.replaceFirst("!", "")
commandHandler.executeCommand(content, event)

}
```

Adding Rich Embeds

To make interactions more engaging, Discord allows the use of rich embeds, which can contain images, fields, and various formatting options.

Here's an example of how to send an embed in response to user commands:

```groovy
import net.dv8tion.jda.api.EmbedBuilder

commandHandler.registerCommand("embed", { event ->
EmbedBuilder embed = new EmbedBuilder()
embed.setTitle("Help Menu")

embed.setDescription("Here are the commands you can use:") embed.addField("!hello", "Sends a greeting message.", false) embed.addField("!embed", "Displays this help menu.", false) embed.setColor(0x00FF00) // Green color
event.channel.sendMessageEmbeds(embed.build()).queue(
)

})
```

Using Reactions

Enhancing user experience can also involve adding reactions to messages. Users appreciate feedback that acknowledges their messages.

You can modify an event to add a reaction after a command is processed:

```groovy
event.message.addReaction("????").queue()
```

Handling User Input and Contextual Responses

For more personalized interactions, consider handling

user input dynamically. This can be done using message context and integrating with an external API or database to fetch user-specific data.

Here's a simple implementation that offers personalized recommendations based on user name:

```groovy
commandHandler.registerCommand("recommend",      { event ->

String userName = event.author.name

event.channel.sendMessage("Hi      $userName!      I recommend you to check out our latest features!").queue()

})
```

Developing engaging and interactive bots on Discord using Groovy is not just feasible but can lead to innovative user experiences. By implementing command handlers, utilizing rich embeds, handling reactions, and personalizing user interactions, you can create a bot that not only responds to commands but also fosters a sense of community.

Chapter 8: Telegram Bot Development

Telegram Bots provide a powerful way to engage with users, automate processes, and create unique experiences within the Telegram ecosystem. In this chapter, we will explore the fundamentals of Telegram bot development, covering the Telegram Bot API, the programming languages and frameworks you can use, and key best practices for creating robust and responsive bots.

Understanding Telegram Bots

Telegram Bots are third-party applications that run inside the Telegram app. They can perform a variety of tasks, such as answering queries, managing groups, sending notifications, or facilitating interactive games. Users can easily interact with these bots by sending commands or messages in a chat, and the bots respond with messages, rich cards, inline keyboards, or more.

Key Features of Telegram Bots:

User Interaction: Bots can respond to user commands by processing messages or inline queries.

Webhooks and Long Polling: Bots can receive updates through webhooks or long polling methods, allowing for real-time interactions.

Rich Media Support: Bots can send various forms of content, including text, images, videos, documents, and audio.

Inline Mode: Bots can work in inline mode, allowing users to invoke them even when typing in a chat, providing instant feedback and results.

Custom Commands: Developers can create custom

commands that users can invoke with a simple slash (/) in the chat.

Setting Up Your Development Environment

Before we dive into writing code, let's set up the environment for Telegram bot development. ### Step 1: Creating a Telegram Bot

Open Telegram: Start by opening the Telegram application.

BotFather: Search for the user "@BotFather" in the Telegram search bar. The BotFather is an official bot provided by Telegram to create and manage other bots.

Creating a New Bot: Start a chat with BotFather and send the command `/newbot`. The BotFather will guide you through the process of naming your bot and creating a unique username (ending with "bot").

Get Your Token: Once the bot is created, BotFather will provide you with a unique API token. This token will allow you to communicate with Telegram's Bot API, so keep it secure.

Step 2: Programming the Bot

You can develop your Telegram bot using various programming languages (Python, JavaScript, Node.js, etc.). In this chapter, we will use Python due to its simplicity and the availability of robust libraries.

Prerequisites

Before you start coding, ensure you have the following installed on your machine:

Python (version 3.x)

pip (Python package installer)

Step 3: Installing Libraries

Use the following command to install the Python package `python-telegram-bot`, which simplifies working with the Telegram Bot API:

```bash
pip install python-telegram-bot
```

Writing Your First Bot

Now, let's write a simple bot that responds to the `/start` command with a welcome message. ### Example Code

Create a new Python file called `my_telegram_bot.py` and add the following code:

```python
import logging

from telegram import Update

from telegram.ext import Updater, CommandHandler, CallbackContext

# Enable logging

logging.basicConfig(format='%(asctime)s - %(name)s - %(levelname)s - %(message)s', level=logging.INFO)

# Define a command handler for the /start command

def start(update: Update, context: CallbackContext) -> None: update.message.reply_text("Welcome to my Telegram bot!")

def main():
```

```python
# Create the Updater and pass it your bot's token
updater = Updater("YOUR_BOT_TOKEN_HERE", use_context=True)

# Get the dispatcher to register handlers dispatcher = updater.dispatcher

# Register the command handler dispatcher.add_handler(CommandHandler("start", start))

# Start the Bot updater.start_polling()

# Run the bot until you send a signal to stop (Ctrl+C) updater.idle()

if __name__ == '__main__':

main()
```

Running the Bot

To run your bot, execute the following command in the terminal:

```bash
python my_telegram_bot.py
```

After you run the script, open Telegram, find your bot using its username, and initiate a chat by sending the command `/start`. Your bot should respond with a welcome message.

Advanced Features

Now that you have a basic bot running, let's explore some

advanced features you can implement. ### 1. Handling Text Messages

Beyond command handling, your bot can respond to text messages. You can create a message handler to manage incoming text:

```python
from telegram.ext import MessageHandler, Filters

def echo(update: Update, context: CallbackContext) -> None: update.message.reply_text(update.message.text)

dispatcher.add_handler(MessageHandler(Filters.text & ~Filters.command, echo))
```

2. Inline Queries

Your bot can respond to inline queries, providing instant results as users type. You can set up an inline query handler to respond to these queries.

3. Rich Media Posts

Learn how to send images, videos, and other media files to enrich the interactions users can have with your bot.

4. Using Webhooks

For production-ready bots, consider using webhooks instead of polling. Webhooks allow Telegram to notify your server when updates occur, enhancing performance and reducing resource consumption.

In this chapter, we've explored the fundamentals of Telegram bot development. Starting from creating a bot through the BotFather to writing simple Python code to respond to user commands, you now have the foundational knowledge to build engaging and functional Telegram bots.

Setting Up a Telegram Bot with Groovy

This chapter will guide you through the steps to set up a Telegram bot using Groovy, a dynamic language for the Java platform. Groovy's syntax is similar to Java but more concise, which makes it an excellent choice for building bots quickly and efficiently.

Prerequisites

Before we dive into the code, make sure you have the following:

Java Development Kit (JDK): Ensure that you have JDK 8 or higher installed on your machine.

Groovy: Install Groovy from http://groovy-lang.org/download.html.

Telegram Account: If you don't already have a Telegram account, download the app and create one. ### Step 1: Create a Telegram Bot

Open Telegram: Launch the Telegram app on your device.

Find the BotFather: In the search bar, type `@BotFather`. BotFather is the official bot for creating new bots on Telegram.

Start a Chat with BotFather: Click on the BotFather to

open a chat and send the command `/start`.

Create a New Bot: To create a new bot, send the command `/newbot`. BotFather will then ask you for a name and a username for your bot:

Name: This is the display name for your bot.

Username: This must end in "bot" (e.g., MySampleBot).

Receive Your Token: Once the bot is created, you will receive a token that will be used to interact with the Telegram Bot API. Save this token; you'll need it later.

Step 2: Set Up Your Groovy Environment

Create a new directory for your project and navigate into it:

```bash
mkdir TelegramGroovyBot cd TelegramGroovyBot
```

Create a `build.gradle` File

The build file helps manage dependencies. Create a `build.gradle` file with the following content:

```groovy
groovy plugins {
id 'groovy'
}
repositories { mavenCentral()

}
```

```
dependencies {

implementation      'org.codehaus.groovy:groovy-all:3.0.9'
implementation
'com.github.badsyntax:telegrambots:5.4.0'

}
```
```

### Step 3: Write Your Bot Code

Create a new Groovy file, `TelegramBot.groovy`, inside your project directory:

```groovy
@Grab(group='org.telegram',      module='telegrambots',
version='5.4.0')                            import
org.telegram.telegrambots.bots.TelegramLongPollingBot

import
org.telegram.telegrambots.meta.annotations.{Configured,
BotCommand,       TelegramBotApp}       import
org.telegram.telegrambots.meta.api.methods.send.SendM
essage

import
org.telegram.telegrambots.meta.api.objects.Update   class
MyTelegramBot extends TelegramLongPollingBot {

def token = "<YOUR_BOT_TOKEN>"

@Override

String getBotUsername() {

return "<YOUR_BOT_USERNAME>"  //  replace  with
your bot username

}
```
```

```java
@Override
String getBotToken() { return token
}
@Override
void onUpdateReceived(Update update) {
if              (update.hasMessage()              &&
update.getMessage().hasText())                    {
handleIncomingMessage(update)
}
}
void handleIncomingMessage(Update update) {
String              chatId              =
update.getMessage().getChatId().toString()        String
messageText = update.getMessage().getText()
SendMessage message = new SendMessage() // Create a
message
.setChatId(chatId)
.setText("You said: " + messageText) // Echo the message
back
try {
execute(message) // Send the message
} catch (Exception e) { e.printStackTrace()
}
}
}
```

```
// Entry point to run the bot @TelegramBotApp
def main(String[] args) {

MyTelegramBot    bot    =    new    MyTelegramBot()
TelegramBotsApi botsApi = new TelegramBotsApi()


try {
botsApi.registerBot(bot)
} catch (Exception e) { e.printStackTrace()
}
}
```
```

Replace            `<YOUR_BOT_TOKEN>`            and
`<YOUR_BOT_USERNAME>` with your specific details
from the BotFather.

### Step 4: Run Your Bot

Compile and run the bot using Gradle:

```bash
./gradlew run
```

You should see no errors in the console, which indicates
that your bot is running. You can now go back to Telegram
and send a message to your bot. The bot should respond
with an echo of your message.

This bot can be the foundation for more complex
functionality such as responding to commands, handling
inline queries, and integrating with various APIs.
```

Experiment with adding commands, processing different types of messages, and even incorporating databases for more advanced features. In the upcoming chapters, we will delve into expanding your bot's capabilities further.

Sending and Receiving Messages Programmatically

This chapter will delve into the various approaches to send and receive messages in Groovy, leveraging libraries, frameworks, and Groovy's native capabilities.

1. Understanding Messaging Concepts

Before we dive into coding examples, it's essential to understand the basic concepts of messaging:

Message: A discrete unit of data that is exchanged between systems or components.

Producer: An entity that sends messages to a message broker or a messaging queue.

Consumer: An entity that receives and processes messages from a queue or a broker.

Messaging can be synchronous or asynchronous. Synchronous messaging waits for a response, while asynchronous messaging allows sending and receiving messages independently.

2. Simple Messaging with Groovy

Groovy provides several ways to send and receive simple messages. One of the most straightforward methods is using HTTP requests. This is particularly useful for interacting with RESTful APIs.

2.1 Sending HTTP Messages

Here is a simple example of sending a message using Groovy's built-in HTTP capabilities:

```groovy
@Grab(group='org.codehaus.gpars',         module='gpars',
version='1.2.1') import groovy.json.JsonOutput

import groovyx.net.http.RESTClient

def sendMessage(def url, def message) { def client = new
RESTClient(url)

def jsonMessage = JsonOutput.toJson(message)   def
response = client.post(

path: '/api/messages',

body:            jsonMessage,           requestContentType:
'application/json'

)

return response

}

def message = [title: 'Test Message', body: 'This is a test
message.']           def           response           =
sendMessage('http://localhost:8080',           message)
println("Response:                  ${response.status}:
${response.data}")
```

In the example above:

We create a function `sendMessage` that takes a URL and a message as parameters.

We convert the message to JSON format using `JsonOutput`.

We use the `RESTClient` to post the message to the specified endpoint. ### 2.2 Receiving HTTP Messages

Receiving messages involves setting up a server that listens for incoming requests. Fortunately, Groovy's built-in capabilities allow us to create a simple server using `HttpServer`.

```groovy
import groovy.json.JsonSlurper

import com.sun.net.httpserver.HttpServer import com.sun.net.httpserver.HttpHandler import com.sun.net.httpserver.HttpExchange

def startServer(int port) {

def server = HttpServer.create(new InetSocketAddress(port), 0) server.createContext("/api/messages", new MessageHandler()) server.start()

println("Server started on port $port")

}

class MessageHandler implements HttpHandler { void handle(HttpExchange exchange) {

def response = "Message received"

if (exchange.requestMethod == "POST") {

def reader = new InputStreamReader(exchange.requestBody) def
```

```
jsonParser = new JsonSlurper()

def message = jsonParser.parse(reader)

println("Received          message:          ${message}")
exchange.sendResponseHeaders(200, response.length())

} else {

response   =   "Only   POST   method   is   supported"
exchange.sendResponseHeaders(405, response.length())

}

exchange.responseBody.write(response.bytes)
exchange.responseBody.close()

}

}

startServer(8080)
```
` ` `

In this server example:

We create an HTTP server that listens on the specified port.

The `MessageHandler` processes incoming POST requests, reads the message, and prints it to the console.
3. Advanced Messaging with Message Brokers

For more scalable and robust messaging, leveraging message brokers like RabbitMQ, Kafka, or ActiveMQ is recommended. These systems facilitate asynchronous messaging using queues.

3.1 Sending Messages with RabbitMQ

Using the RabbitMQ library in Groovy makes it easy to

send messages to a queue:

```groovy
@Grab('org.rabbitmq:amqp-client:5.9.0')                    import
com.rabbitmq.client.*

def    sendRabbitMessage(String    queueName,    String
message) { def factory = new ConnectionFactory()

factory.host = 'localhost'

try (Connection  connection  =  factory.newConnection();
Channel    channel    =    connection.createChannel())    {
channel.queueDeclare(queueName, false, false, false, null)

channel.basicPublish('', queueName, null, message.bytes)
println("Sent: '${message}'")

}
}
sendRabbitMessage('hello', 'Hello, RabbitMQ!')
```

3.2 Receiving Messages with RabbitMQ

To receive messages from a RabbitMQ queue, you would
create a consumer:

```groovy
def  receiveRabbitMessages(String  queueName)  {  def
factory  =  new  ConnectionFactory()  factory.host  =
'localhost'

try (Connection  connection  =  factory.newConnection();
Channel    channel    =    connection.createChannel())    {
```

```
channel.queueDeclare(queueName, false, false, false, null)
def deliverCallback = { consumerTag, delivery ->
println("Received: '${new String(delivery.body)}'")
}

channel.basicConsume(queueName, true, deliverCallback,
{ consumerTag -> })
}
}
receiveRabbitMessages('hello')
```
```
```

Chapter 9: Advanced Groovy Scripting Techniques

In this chapter, we will focus on several advanced Groovy scripting techniques that can help you write more efficient, maintainable, and expressive code. Key topics include closures, metaprogramming, DSLs (Domain-Specific Languages), and the use of the Groovy ecosystem to leverage third-party libraries and tools. By mastering these advanced concepts, you will enhance your ability to solve complex programming challenges in a more elegant manner.

1. Closures and Functional Programming

Groovy's closure is a powerful feature that enables functions to be treated as first-class citizens. Closures are anonymous blocks of code that can be assigned to variables, passed as arguments, and returned from methods. Their versatility makes them a fundamental construct in Groovy.

1.1 Defining and Using Closures

You can define a closure using curly braces. The simplest example is:

```groovy
def greet = { name -> "Hello, $name!" }

println greet("World")  // Output: Hello, World!
```

Closures can take parameters, and you can also access variables from the surrounding scope thanks to Groovy's lexical scoping.

1.2 Closures with Collection Methods

Groovy collections support a variety of methods that take closures, which makes data transformation and filtering more intuitive. For example:

```groovy
def numbers = [1, 2, 3, 4, 5]
def squaredNumbers = numbers.collect { it * it } println squaredNumbers // Output: [1, 4, 9, 16, 25]
```

Here, we use the `collect` method to apply a closure to each element in the list, transforming it in an elegant and concise manner.

2. Metaprogramming in Groovy

Metaprogramming allows you to modify classes, methods, and properties at runtime. This powerful technique can be used to add dynamic behavior to your scripts and to enhance flexibility.

2.1 The `Expando` Class

The `Expando` class is a great starting point for metaprogramming in Groovy. It allows you to create objects whose properties and methods can be added at runtime.

```groovy
def person = new Expando() person.name = 'John'
person.greet = { -> "Hello, I'm $name" }
```

```
println person.greet() // Output: Hello, I'm John
```

In this snippet, we create a dynamically-defined object and add properties and methods to it on the fly. ### 2.2 Intercepting Method Calls

Using the `MetaClass`, you can intercept method calls for dynamic method resolution. This allows for advanced scenarios such as proxying behavior or enhancing existing methods.

```groovy
String.metaClass.toUpperCase = { -> "Intercepted: ${delegate.toLowerCase()}" } println "hello".toUpperCase() // Output: Intercepted: hello
```

This example overrides the `toUpperCase` method for the `String` class. When called, the new behavior is invoked instead of the original method.

3. Building Domain-Specific Languages (DSLs)

Groovy excels at creating DSLs due to its flexible syntax and ease of manipulation. DSLs allow you to express domain concepts with clarity and brevity.

3.1 Creating a Simple DSL

Consider a configuration DSL for a hypothetical web application:

```groovy
def webApp = {
appName "My Cool App" environment "production"
```

```groovy
database {
url "jdbc:mysql://localhost:3306/mydb" user "admin"
password "secret"
}
}
webApp()
```

This DSL reflects a configuration structure intuitively, which is easy for developers to read and understand. ### 3.2 Implementing a Builder

Building a DSL often involves employing Groovy's `Builder` class. This provides a more structured approach to creating hierarchical objects.

```groovy
class HtmlBuilder {


def writer = new StringWriter()
def invokeMethod(String name, def args) { writer << "<$name>${args.join("")}</$name>"
}
}
def html = new HtmlBuilder() html.html {
head {
title "My Page"
}
```

```
body {
h1 "Welcome"
p "This is a paragraph."
}
}
println html.writer.toString()
```

In this example, we create an HTML structure using a Groovy Builder, intuitively nesting elements inside each other.

4. Integrating with the Groovy Ecosystem

Groovy has a rich ecosystem that offers numerous libraries and frameworks. Learning to integrate with these tools will dramatically enhance your scripting capabilities.

4.1 Leveraging Grape for Dependency Management

Grape is Groovy's built-in dependency management tool. It allows you to add external libraries easily:

```groovy
@Grab(group='org.apache.commons', module='commons-lang3', version='3.12.0') import org.apache.commons.lang3.StringUtils

def result = StringUtils.capitalize("hello") println result // Output: Hello
```

This snippet demonstrates how to fetch an external library seamlessly while writing Groovy scripts. ### 4.2 Utilizing

Testing Frameworks

Groovy integrates well with testing frameworks like Spock and Geb. These tools can help you write robust tests for your applications, improving code quality and maintainability.

```groovy
import spock.lang.Specification

class MySpec extends Specification { def "basic math"() {

expect:


1 + 1 == 2
}
}
```

Spock's expressive syntax for writing tests provides clarity and enhances the development process.

By understanding closures, metaprogramming, building DSLs, and integrating with the Groovy ecosystem, you can write more powerful and efficient scripts that are not only effective but also elegant. These techniques allow you to push the boundaries of what you can achieve with Groovy, empowering you to tackle more sophisticated challenges in your development journey. As you continue to practice and apply these methods, you will find that the simplicity and dynamism of Groovy truly unleash your creativity in the world of programming.

Streamlining Your Code with Closures and DSLs

This chapter explores the essence of closures and DSLs in Groovy, showcasing how these concepts can streamline your code, making it more expressive and easier to manage.

Understanding Closures

Closures are a distinct feature in Groovy, allowing you to define a block of code that can be executed later. Closures are first-class citizens in Groovy, meaning you can pass them around as parameters, store them in variables, and even return them from methods. A closure can capture the surrounding context (variables and state) in which it is defined, leading to powerful abstraction capabilities.

Defining a Closure

A simple closure in Groovy is defined using curly braces `{}`. Here's how you might define a closure to return the sum of two numbers:

```groovy
def sum = { num1, num2 -> num1 + num2 } println sum(5, 10) // Outputs: 15
```

In this example, `sum` is a closure that takes two parameters, `num1` and `num2`, and returns their sum. You can invoke this closure like a regular method, showcasing Groovy's flexibility.

Closures with Context

One of the strengths of closures is their ability to capture the surrounding context, including variables that are defined outside the closure. Consider the following example:

```groovy
def multiplier = 2

def timesTwo = { num -> num * multiplier } println timesTwo(5) // Outputs: 10
```

Here, the closure `timesTwo` captures the `multiplier` variable, enabling it to use it whenever it's invoked. This behavior allows for more modular code and reduces the need for managing state through cumbersome object properties.

Closures for Collection Manipulation

Groovy's collection methods are heavily reliant on closures, allowing for concise and expressive manipulation of data structures. You can use closures to filter, transform, or iterate over collections seamlessly.

```groovy
def numbers = [1, 2, 3, 4, 5]

def doubled = numbers.collect { it * 2 } println doubled // Outputs: [2, 4, 6, 8, 10]
```

In this example, the `collect` method applies the closure to each element of the `numbers` list, effectively doubling each value and returning a new list. Such operations would require verbose loops in other languages, but Groovy makes it concise and readable.

Introducing Domain-Specific Languages (DSLs)

Groovy shines not only with closures but also with its ability to create Domain-Specific Languages (DSLs). A DSL is a specialized language tailored to a specific domain or problem area, providing abstractions that are more intuitive for that domain. Groovy's flexibility allows developers to create DSLs that resemble natural language, enhancing code readability.

Creating a Simple DSL

Let's consider an example of creating a simple DSL for defining tasks. This might be useful for a task management application:

```groovy
class Task {
String name String description
String toString() {
return "[Task: $name, Description: $description]"
}
}
def taskList = []
def task(String name, Closure closure) { def t = new Task(name: name) closure.delegate = t
closure() taskList << t
}
task('Write Documentation') {
description = 'Document the code for better understanding'
```

```
}
task('Implement Feature X') {
description = 'Develop Feature X using Groovy'
}
println taskList
```
```

In this DSL, the `task` method allows you to define tasks in a natural way. The closure passed to the `task` method modifies the `Task` object's properties, enhancing both simplicity and readability. As you can see, this syntax mimics plain English and conveys the intent much more clearly than traditional coding patterns.

### Chaining DSL Methods

DSLs can also leverage method chaining to create fluent APIs. The following example enhances the task definition by allowing for method chaining:

```groovy
class Task {
String name String description
Task setDescription(String desc) { this.description = desc
return this
}
String toString() {
return "[Task: $name, Description: $description]"
}
```
```

```
}
def taskList = []

def task(String name, Closure closure) { def t = new
Task(name: name) closure.delegate = t

closure() taskList << t

}
task('Write Tests') {

setDescription('Write unit tests for all functionalities')

}
task('Review Code') {

setDescription('Review the implementation and provide
feedback')

}
println taskList
```
` ` `

This method chaining allows you to call `setDescription`
directly, resulting in a more fluid interaction with the
`Task` objects while still maintaining a clear and concise
syntax.

In this chapter, we explored the concepts of closures and
Domain-Specific Languages in Groovy. By harnessing
closures, developers can write modular, concise, and
readable code while focusing on the intent rather than the
implementation details. DSLs take this a step further,
allowing for the creation of expressive syntax tailored to
specific domains, greatly enhancing code clarity.

Handling Errors and Debugging Chatbot Scripts

This chapter delves into the methodologies and best practices for managing errors and debugging in Groovy, ensuring that your chatbots perform as expected.

1. Understanding Common Errors in Chatbot Development

Before we delve into error handling, it is crucial to understand the types of errors that can occur in chatbot development:

1.1 Syntax Errors

Syntax errors occur when the code does not conform to the required syntax. In Groovy, this could be a missing parenthesis, an incorrect variable declaration, or an improperly closed string.

1.2 Runtime Errors

These errors happen during the execution of the script. For example, trying to access a null object can lead to a `NullPointerException`. They can be tricky because the script may compile successfully but fail when run.

1.3 Logic Errors

Logic errors are more subtle; the code runs without crashing, but it produces incorrect results due to flawed logic. These can stem from incorrect algorithms, data handling, or flow control.

2. Implementing Error Handling in Groovy

Groovy provides a robust mechanism for error handling through exception handling constructs. Understanding how to utilize these will help maintain the user experience and ensure graceful degradation when errors occur.

2.1 Try-Catch Blocks

Using `try-catch` blocks allows developers to catch exceptions and handle them appropriately. Here's an example code snippet:

```groovy
def executeChatbotLogic(input) { try {

// Process user input

def response = processInput(input) return response

} catch (NullPointerException e) {

logError("A null value was encountered: ${e.message}") return "I'm sorry, something went wrong on our end."

} catch (Exception e) {

logError("An unexpected error occurred: ${e.message}") return "I encountered an error. Please try again later."

}

}
```

Here, we log specific errors while providing the user with a general message, maintaining the chatbot's usability.

2.2 Finally Block

A `finally` block can be used if there is cleanup that needs to occur regardless of whether an exception was thrown.

```groovy
def executeChatbotLogic(input) { try {

// Process user input

def response = processInput(input) return response

} catch (Exception e) {

logError("An error occurred: ${e.message}") return "An error occurred, please try again."

} finally {

// Cleanup tasks, such as closing connections cleanupResources()

}

}
```

3. Debugging Techniques for Groovy Scripts

Debugging is the process of identifying and resolving errors within your scripts. Here are some effective techniques specifically catered to Groovy.

3.1 Logging

Implementing proper logging is essential for debugging. Using frameworks such as Log4j or SLF4J can help you keep track of application flow and identify where errors occur.

```groovy
import org.slf4j.Logger
```

```groovy
import org.slf4j.LoggerFactory

class Chatbot {

private static final Logger logger = LoggerFactory.getLogger(Chatbot.class)

def handleUserInput(input) { logger.info("Received input: {}", input) try {

// Chatbot logic

} catch (Exception e) {

logger.error("Error handling input: {}", input, e)

}

}

}
```

3.2 Unit Testing

Creating unit tests for your chatbot logic can greatly minimize the chance of errors. Groovy provides testing libraries such as Spock, which makes writing tests easy and effective. Here's an example:

```groovy
import spock.lang.Specification


class ChatbotTest extends Specification {

def "test chatbot response"() { expect:

chatbot.handleUserInput("Hello") == "Hello! How can I assist you today?"
```

151

```
}
}
```
```
` ` `
```

3.3 Using an Integrated Development Environment (IDE)

Make use of IDEs like IntelliJ IDEA or Eclipse with Groovy support. These environments offer rich debugging features such as breakpoints, variable watches, and call stack inspection, allowing for more efficient tracking of issues.

3.4 Profiling

For performance-related issues, profiling your scripts can help identify bottlenecks. Tools like Java VisualVM or Groovy-specific profilers will provide insights into resource usage and performance.

4. Best Practices for Writing Robust Chatbot Scripts
4.1 Write Clean, Maintainable Code

Use clear variable names, good indentation, and comment on complex sections of your code. This will help

identify logical errors when reviewing or modifying code.

4.2 Implement Graceful Degradation

Always anticipate potential failures. Provide fallback messages or alternative actions when the primary response fails.

4.3 Monitor and Iterate

After deployment, don't assume the bot will function perfectly. Monitor performance and user interactions to refine the script continuously.

By understanding different types of errors, implementing proper error handling mechanisms, utilizing robust debugging techniques, and adhering to best practices, developers can create resilient chatbots that enhance user experience and maintain operational integrity. With these skills in your toolkit, you are well-equipped to tackle challenges and deliver effective chatbot solutions.

Chapter 10: Enhancing Bot Intelligence with APIs

One key aspect that enhances a bot's intelligence is its ability to connect and interact with external systems, datasets, and services—this is where APIs (Application Programming Interfaces) play a crucial role. In this chapter, we will explore how to enhance the intelligence of bots using APIs with Groovy, a versatile scripting language that simplifies the process of integrating with various services.

10.1 Understanding APIs in the Context of Bots

APIs allow different software programs to communicate with one another. In the context of bots, they serve as gateways to access external data, functionalities, or services, which can significantly increase what your bot can do. When bots interact with APIs, they can:

Retrieve real-time data (e.g., weather, news, stock prices).

Send and receive messages from other platforms (e.g., Slack, Telegram).

Perform calculations or data transformations using remote services.

Access databases and manipulate data on the fly.

The use of APIs transforms static bots into dynamic, responsive entities that can learn and adapt based on external input.

10.2 Setting Up Your Groovy Environment

Before we dive into coding, let's set up a basic environment to develop our Groovy scripts. Groovy is built on Java, making it compatible with existing Java libraries while providing a syntax that is easier to read and write.

Install Groovy:

If you haven't installed Groovy yet, download and install it from the [official Groovy website](https://groovy-lang.org/).

Ensure your environment variables are set up correctly to run Groovy from the command line.

Integrated Development Environment (IDE):

While you can use any text editor, IDEs like IntelliJ IDEA or Eclipse provide additional functionality such as code completion, project management, and debugging tools.

10.3 Making HTTP Requests with Groovy

To interact with APIs, you typically send HTTP requests using methods such as GET, POST, PUT, and DELETE. Groovy makes it easy to perform these operations with its simplified syntax.

Example: Fetching Weather Data

In this example, we will fetch weather data from a third-party API. We'll use the OpenWeatherMap API for our demonstration.

Sign Up for API Key:

- First, create an account and get your free API key from [OpenWeatherMap](https://openweathermap.org/api).

Write the Groovy Script:

```groovy
```

```groovy
@Grab(group='org.codehaus.gpars',    module='gpars',
version='1.4.0')

import        groovy.json.JsonSlurper        import
groovyx.net.http.RESTClient

def getWeather(city) {

def apiKey = 'YOUR_API_KEY' // Replace with your API
Key            def            baseURL            =
'http://api.openweathermap.org/data/2.5/weather'

def client = new RESTClient(baseURL)

def response = client.get(path: '', query: [q: city, appid:
apiKey]) if(response.status == 200) {

def json = new JsonSlurper().parseText(response.data)
return json

} else {

println        "Error:        ${response.status}        -
${response.statusLine}" return null

}

}

def weatherData = getWeather('London') if (weatherData)
{

println    "Weather    in    ${weatherData.name}:
${weatherData.weather[0].description}, Temp:

${weatherData.main.temp - 273.15}°C"

}
```
```

In this script, we use Groovy's `@Grab` annotation to
```

include the GPars library for handling concurrent tasks elegantly. We then create a REST client that performs a GET request to the OpenWeatherMap API, parses the JSON response, and prints out the weather information in a readable format.

10.4 Enhancing Bot Capabilities

Now that we can fetch data from an API, let's consider how to integrate this functionality into a bot context. By enhancing our bot with API capabilities, it can:

Provide users with instant weather updates.

Answer queries related to current events by fetching news headlines.

Access user data from a database or analytics service to enhance personalization. #### Example: Bot Integration

Consider a simple scenario where our Groovy bot provides weather updates when users ask for them.

```groovy
def botResponse(userInput) {

if (userInput.toLowerCase().contains('weather')) {

def weatherData = getWeather('London') // You could make it dynamic based on user input if (weatherData) {

return "The weather in ${weatherData.name} is ${weatherData.weather[0].description} with a temperature of ${weatherData.main.temp - 273.15}°C."


} else {

return "Sorry, I couldn't fetch the weather data right now."
```

157

```
    }
  }
  return "I'm not sure how to respond to that!"
}
// Simulated User Input
println botResponse("What's the weather like?")
```

10.5 Best Practices for API Integration

When integrating APIs into your bot, consider the following best practices:

Rate Limiting: Be aware of the rate limits imposed by the API providers. Too many requests in a short period can lead to your bot being blocked.

Error Handling: Always implement error handling to manage API failures gracefully. This will enhance the user experience by providing thoughtful feedback.

Caching Responses: To minimize API calls and improve response time, consider caching frequently requested data.

Security: Store sensitive information, like API keys, securely. Avoid hard-coding them into your scripts.

User Input Validation: When making API calls based on user input, ensure you validate and sanitize inputs to prevent issues.

The simplicity of Groovy allows developers to implement

these features with ease, paving the way for building more sophisticated and intelligent conversational agents. As you continue your journey in bot development, remember that APIs are powerful tools that, when used effectively, can unlock endless possibilities for your projects.

Connecting to AI APIs (e.g., OpenAI, Dialogflow)

Leveraging AI APIs, such as OpenAI's models for natural language processing or Google's Dialogflow for conversational interfaces, has never been easier. This chapter will guide you through the process of connecting to these powerful APIs using Groovy, a versatile and dynamic language that runs on the Java Virtual Machine (JVM).

Understanding API Key Management

Before you can utilize any AI API, you'll need to understand how to manage your API keys. Both OpenAI and Google Cloud (which offers Dialogflow) require API keys for authentication. Here's how to manage your API keys securely:

Obtain API Keys:

For OpenAI, sign up at their [official website](https://openai.com/) and follow their instructions to generate an API key.

For Dialogflow, create a Google Cloud project, enable the Dialogflow API, and then generate a service account key or API key.

Security Measures:

Store your API keys in a secure location. Avoid hardcoding them in your source code. Instead, consider using environment variables or configuration files that are not included in version control.

Setting Up Groovy Environment

Before diving into the code, ensure you have a Groovy environment set up. If you haven't already, download and install Groovy from the [Groovy website](https://groovy-lang.org/download.html). You can also use a build tool like Gradle or Maven, which can help manage dependencies.

Sample Groovy Setup with Gradle

If you're using Gradle, create a `build.gradle` file in your project directory:

```groovy
plugins {
id 'groovy'
}
repositories { mavenCentral()
}
dependencies {
implementation 'org.codehaus.groovy:groovy-all:3.0.9'
implementation 'com.squareup.okhttp3:okhttp:4.9.1'
    // HTTP client for API calls implementation 'com.google.code.gson:gson:2.8.6'     // For JSON parsing
}
```

Making HTTP Requests to OpenAI API

To connect to the OpenAI API, you will need to make HTTP requests. For the purpose of this example, we will create a class that interfaces with OpenAI's language model endpoint.

Example Code: OpenAI API Integration

```groovy
import okhttp3.*

import com.google.gson.JsonObject
import com.google.gson.JsonParser

class OpenAIClient {

private static final String OPENAI_API_URL = "https://api.openai.com/v1/completions" private String apiKey

OpenAIClient(String apiKey) { this.apiKey = apiKey

}

String generateResponse(String prompt) { OkHttpClient client = new OkHttpClient()

JsonObject json = new JsonObject()

json.addProperty("model", "text-davinci-003") // Example model json.addProperty("prompt", prompt) json.addProperty("max_tokens", 100)

RequestBody body = RequestBody.create( MediaType.get("application/json; charset=utf-8"), json.toString()
)

Request request = new Request.Builder()
```

```
.url(OPENAI_API_URL)

.post(body)

.addHeader("Authorization", "Bearer $apiKey")

.build()

try (Response response = client.newCall(request).execute()) { if (!response.isSuccessful()) {

throw new IOException("Unexpected code $response")

}

// Parse the response

JsonObject responseBody = JsonParser.parseString(response.body().string()).getAsJsonObject() return

responseBody.getAsJsonArray("choices").get(0).getAsJsonObject().get("text").getAsString().trim()

}

}

}
```
` ` `

Usage Example

` ` `groovy

```
def apiClient = new OpenAIClient("YOUR_OPENAI_API_KEY")

def response = apiClient.generateResponse("What are the benefits of AI in healthcare?")
```

```groovy
println response
```

Connecting to Dialogflow for Conversational AI

Integrating with Dialogflow allows you to create chatbots that can understand and respond to user input in a natural manner. To connect to Dialogflow using Groovy, you must also perform HTTP requests, similar to the OpenAI integration.

Example Code: Dialogflow API Integration

```groovy
class DialogflowClient {

private static final String DIALOGFLOW_URL = "https://dialogflow.googleapis.com/v2/projects/YOUR_PROJECT_ID/agent/sessions/YOUR_SESSION_ID:detectIn

private String accessToken

DialogflowClient(String accessToken) { this.accessToken = accessToken
}

String detectIntent(String query) { OkHttpClient client = new OkHttpClient()

JsonObject json = new JsonObject()
json.addProperty("queryInput",

new JsonObject().addProperty("text", new JsonObject().addProperty("text",
query).addProperty("languageCode", "en")).toString())

RequestBody body = RequestBody.create(
```

```
MediaType.get("application/json;          charset=utf-8"),
json.toString()
)
Request request = new Request.Builder()
.url(DIALOGFLOW_URL)
.post(body)
.addHeader("Authorization", "Bearer $accessToken")
.build()
try          (Response          response          =
client.newCall(request).execute())          {          if
(!response.isSuccessful()) {
throw new IOException("Unexpected code $response")
}
JsonObject          responseBody          =
JsonParser.parseString(response.body().string()).getAsJs
onObject()          return
responseBody.getAsJsonObject("queryResult").get("fulfill
mentText").getAsString()
}
}
}
```

Usage Example
```groovy
def          dialogflowClient          =          new
DialogflowClient("YOUR_DIALOGFLOW_ACCESS_TOK
```

EN")

```
def response = dialogflowClient.detectIntent("Hello, how
can you help me?") println response
```
` ` `

By following the examples provided in this chapter, you can effectively connect to both OpenAI and Dialogflow APIs. As you experiment with these technologies, consider exploring advancements in AI models and enhancing your application's capabilities further. Always remember to adhere to best practices regarding API usage and security to ensure your applications remain performant and secure.

Adding NLP Capabilities to Your Groovy Chatbots

This chapter explores how to integrate NLP capabilities into your Groovy chatbots, empowering them to deliver richer, more effective conversations with users.

Understanding NLP Basics

Before diving into the implementation, it's essential to grasp the fundamental concepts of NLP. At its core, NLP encompasses various techniques that enable computers to process and analyze vast amounts of language data. Here are some key components:

Tokenization: Breaking down sentences into manageable pieces called tokens (words or phrases).

Part-of-Speech Tagging: Identifying the grammatical

parts of each token, such as noun, verb, or adjective.

Named Entity Recognition (NER): Spotting and categorizing key entities in text, such as names, dates, or locations.

Sentiment Analysis: Analyzing the tone or sentiment of the text to determine if it is positive, negative, or neutral.

Intent Recognition: Understanding the user's intent based on their input to provide appropriate responses.

Why NLP for Chatbots?

Integrating NLP into your Groovy chatbots provides several advantages, including:

Improved User Experience: Natural interactions foster a better user experience, enabling users to communicate in a more conversational manner rather than resorting to rigid command structures.

Context Awareness: NLP capabilities allow chatbots to maintain context over multiple exchanges, making the conversation more fluid and coherent.

Personalization: By analyzing user input, chatbots can tailor responses based on individual preferences, enhancing the perceived value of interactions.

Setting Up Your Development Environment

Before you can dive into adding NLP capabilities, ensure you have a suitable development environment:

Install Groovy: Ensure you have the latest version of Groovy installed on your machine. You can download it from the [Groovy website](https://groovy-lang.org/download.html).

Choose an NLP Library: Several powerful NLP libraries can be integrated with Groovy to enhance your chatbot's capabilities:

Stanford NLP: A comprehensive suite of tools for NLP but may require Java interop.

OpenNLP: An Apache project that provides various NLP tools suitable for different tasks.

spaCy: While not directly usable in Groovy, you can build a RESTful service in Python and call it from your Groovy application.

Set Up Your Project: Create a new Groovy project, and add dependencies for the chosen NLP library in your build file (e.g., Gradle or Maven).

Implementing NLP in Your Chatbot ### Step 1: Text Preprocessing

Before you can analyze user inputs, you need to preprocess the text. Here's a simple example in Groovy:

```groovy
def preprocessInput(String userInput) {
// Convert to lowercase
userInput = userInput.toLowerCase()

// Remove punctuation
userInput = userInput.replaceAll(/[^\w\s]/, ")
```

```groovy
// Split into tokens
def tokens = userInput.split(/\s+/) return tokens
}
```

Step 2: Intent Recognition

Once the input is preprocessed, you can implement intent recognition. The idea is to classify user input into predefined intents. Here's a simple implementation using keyword matching:

```groovy
def recognizeIntent(String userInput) { def intents = [
'greeting': ['hello', 'hi', 'hey'],
'farewell': ['bye', 'goodbye', 'see you'],
'help': ['help', 'support', 'assist']
]
def tokens = preprocessInput(userInput) intents.each {
intent, keywords ->
tokens.each { token ->
if (keywords.contains(token)) { return intent
}
}
}
return 'unknown'
}
```

```
```

Step 3: Response Generation

After recognizing the intent, generate a suitable response:

```groovy
def generateResponse(String intent) { switch (intent) {
case 'greeting':
return "Hello! How can I assist you today?" case 'farewell':
return "Goodbye! Have a great day!" case 'help':
return "I'm here to help. What do you need assistance with?" default:
return "I'm sorry, I didn't quite understand that."
}
}
```

Step 4: Putting It All Together

Combine the above functions to create a simple chatbot interaction loop:

```groovy
def chatbotInteraction(String userInput) { def intent = recognizeIntent(userInput)    def    response    = generateResponse(intent) return response
}
// Example Usage
println        chatbotInteraction("Hello")        println chatbotInteraction("I need help")
```

```
println chatbotInteraction("See you soon")
```
```

## Advanced NLP Features

As you gain confidence with basic NLP capabilities, you can expand your chatbot further by:

**Integrating Machine Learning Models**: Use pre-trained models for more advanced intent recognition and NER. Frameworks like TensorFlow and PyTorch can be used in conjunction with your Groovy chatbot by calling external services.

**Implementing Dialogue Management**: Create a state machine or use libraries that facilitate more complex multi-turn conversations, keeping track of user queries and context.

**Sentiment Analysis**: Implement a sentiment analysis feature to better gauge user emotions and adjust responses accordingly.

**External APIs**: Leverage APIs like Google Cloud Natural Language, AWS Comprehend, or even Dialogflow for enhanced NLP features, reducing the complexity of your chatbot's training and accuracy precision.

Adding NLP capabilities to your Groovy chatbots doesn't have to be daunting. With some foundational knowledge of NLP concepts, a solid development setup, and some Groovy code examples, you can significantly enhance your chatbots' ability to understand and interact naturally with users.
```

Chapter 11: Customizing Chatbot Workflows

While many platforms offer pre-built chatbot frameworks, the real power lies in customization. In this chapter, we'll explore how to leverage the Groovy programming language to create and customize chatbot workflows that align with your specific needs and use cases.

Introduction to Groovy for Chatbots

Groovy is a powerful, agile scripting language that runs on the Java platform. It provides syntax that is both easy to understand and comprehend, making it an excellent choice for developers looking to customize chatbot functionalities. With its dynamic nature, Groovy allows for swift adjustments and rapid prototyping, essential for any chatbot development project.

In this chapter, we will cover:

Understanding Chatbot Workflows: What they are and why they matter.

Setting Up Your Groovy Environment: Tools and libraries you need.

Defining Custom Workflows: Strategies for workflow management.

Integrating APIs and External Services: Making your chatbot more functional.

Debugging and Testing: Ensuring your workflows are smooth.

Real-World Examples: Implementing your learnings in a practical way. ### Section 1: Understanding Chatbot

Workflows

A chatbot workflow is essentially the series of steps a bot takes to process user input and respond accordingly. Effective workflows can enhance the user experience by minimizing friction and maximizing engagement. Workflows can range from simple question-and-answer patterns to complex interactions requiring decision trees and contextual awareness.

Key Components of a Chatbot Workflow

User Input: What the user says or types.

Intents: The purpose behind the user's input.

Entities: Specific pieces of information that provide context.

Responses: How the bot replies to the user.

Context Management: Tracking the conversation's state to provide relevant responses. ### Section 2: Setting Up Your Groovy Environment

To begin customizing your chatbot workflows using Groovy, you'll need to set up a development environment. Here's how to get started:

Install Groovy: Download and install Groovy from the [official website](https://groovy-lang.org/download.html). Follow the installation guide for your operating system.

Integrated Development Environment (IDE): Use an IDE like IntelliJ IDEA or Eclipse with Groovy support to ease the development process.

Chatbot Framework: Depending on your requirements, choose a chatbot framework that supports Groovy. Options might include Rasa, Botpress, or a custom-built Java-based solution that integrates Groovy.

Required Libraries: Familiarize yourself with libraries such as Grails for web applications or Spock for testing to assist in building robust workflows.

Section 3: Defining Custom Workflows

Once your environment is ready, start building your chatbot workflows. Using Groovy, you can create custom scripts that define how the chatbot processes user input. Here's a simple example:

```groovy
class ChatbotWorkflow { def intents = [:]

def context = [:]

void addIntent(String intentName, Closure action) {
intents[intentName] = action

}

void processInput(String userInput) {

def matchedIntent = intents.find {
userInput.contains(it.key) } if(matchedIntent) {

context['lastIntent'] = matchedIntent.key
matchedIntent.value.call(userInput)

} else {

println("I'm not sure how to respond to that.")

}
```

```
}
}
// Example usage
def     chatbot     =     new     ChatbotWorkflow()
chatbot.addIntent("greet") { input ->
println("Hello! How can I assist you today?")
}
chatbot.processInput("Hi there")
```

Section 4: Integrating APIs and External Services

One of the most powerful features of customizing workflows in Groovy is the ability to integrate external APIs and services. This allows your chatbot to pull in real-time data or trigger actions in other applications. For example, integrating a weather API to provide users with weather updates can be done as follows:

```groovy
import groovy.json.JsonSlurper import java.net.URL

def getWeather(String location) { def apiKey = "your_api_key"

def     url     =     new
URL("http://api.weatherapi.com/v1/current.json?key=${apiKey}&q=${location}")     def     response     =     new
JsonSlurper().parse(url)

return "The current temperature in ${location} is ${response.current.temp_c}°C."
```

```groovy
}
chatbot.addIntent("weather") { input ->

def location = input.split(" ").last() // Simple extraction
def          weatherInfo          =          getWeather(location)
println(weatherInfo)


}
```

Section 5: Debugging and Testing

Debugging and testing are critical stages in the development process to ensure that your workflows are functioning as expected. Groovy leverages JUnit and Spock for testing. You can create test cases for your workflows as shown:

```groovy
import spock.lang.Specification

class ChatbotWorkflowTest extends Specification { def "should respond to greetings"() {

given:

def      chatbot      =      new      ChatbotWorkflow()
chatbot.addIntent("greet") { input -> return "Hello!" }

when:

def response = chatbot.processInput("Hi")

then:

response == "Hello!"

}
```

```
}
```
```
` ` `
```

Section 6: Real-World Examples

The true power of customizing chatbot workflows in Groovy comes from real-world applications. Consider the following scenarios:

Customer Support Bot: A bot that guides users through troubleshooting steps based on their individual issues, using dynamic workflows tailored to previous interactions.

E-commerce Assistant: A chatbot that helps users find products, provides recommendations based on browsing history, and assists in order tracking through various APIs.

By applying customization and integrating with various services, Groovy empowers developers to create chatbots that enrich the user experience by making them more interactive, responsive, and contextually aware.

As we conclude this chapter on customizing chatbot workflows in Groovy, we've explored the foundational elements needed to design, build, and iterate on intelligent conversational experiences.

Using Groovy for Conditional Logic and Dynamic Responses

A well-designed chatbot is not only capable of understanding and responding to queries but also adapting dynamically to various user inputs. Groovy, a powerful scripting language that runs on the Java platform, offers a versatile approach to implementing conditional logic and crafting dynamic responses in chatbot development. This chapter explores the capabilities of Groovy in chatbot design, focusing on how to harness its features for more intelligent conversational agents.

1. Understanding Groovy Basics

Before diving into the implementation of conditional logic, it's essential to grasp the foundational elements of Groovy. Groovy features a concise syntax and supports both object-oriented and functional programming paradigms. Its seamless integration with Java libraries allows developers to leverage existing Java code alongside Groovy scripts. The language's dynamic typing and built-in support for lists, maps, and closures provide the flexibility needed for handling various user interactions.

1.1 Setting Up the Environment

To get started with Groovy for chatbot development, ensure that you have the Groovy environment set up:

Install Groovy: You can download and install Groovy from its official website or use package managers like SDKMAN! for Linux or Homebrew for macOS.

Choose a Development Environment: Popular IDEs like IntelliJ IDEA, Eclipse, or even simple text editors can be used to write Groovy scripts.

Integrate with a Chatbot Framework: Many

frameworks such as Rasa, Botpress, or even Dialogflow can be leveraged alongside Groovy to enhance their capabilities with custom scripts.

2. Implementing Conditional Logic

Conditional logic allows chatbots to make decisions based on user inputs, historical data, and contextual information. Groovy's `if-else` statements, `switch` constructs, and powerful closure capabilities enable dynamic decision-making processes.

2.1 Using `if-else` Statements

The simplest form of conditional logic is the `if-else` statement. Here's a simple example where we classify user inputs:

```groovy
def userInput = "What are your store hours?"

if (userInput.contains("store hours")) {

return "Our store is open from 9 AM to 9 PM."

} else if (userInput.contains("location")) { return "We are located at 123 Main St."

} else {

return "I'm sorry, I didn't understand that."

}
```

In this example, the bot checks user input for keywords to provide a tailored response. ### 2.2 Using `switch` Statements

For more complex scenarios with multiple conditions, `switch` statements can help streamline the logic:

```groovy
def userInput = "I need assistance with my order."

switch (userInput) {

case { it.contains("order") }:

return "Can you please provide your order number?" case { it.contains("return") }:

return "You can return items within 30 days of purchase." default:

return "How can I assist you today?"

}
```

This structure increases readability and manageability of the code while allowing for more extensive conditional checks.

2.3 Using Closures for Dynamic Responses

Groovy supports closures, which can be used to encapsulate blocks of code. This feature can be leveraged to implement dynamic responses based on more complex logic, allowing for modular and reusable components in chatbot development.

```groovy
def responses = [

{ userInput -> userInput.contains("hi") ? "Hello! How can I help you?" : null },
```

```groovy
{ userInput -> userInput.contains("help") ? "Sure! What do you need help with?" : null },

{ userInput -> userInput.contains("bye") ? "Goodbye! Have a great day!" : null }
]
def getResponse(userInput) {

def response = responses.collect { it(userInput) }.find { it != null } return response ?: "I'm not sure how to respond to that."

}
def userInput = "I need some help."

println(getResponse(userInput)) // Output: "Sure! What do you need help with?"
```

In this case, we create a list of responses stored as closures and then dynamically evaluate them based on user input.

3. Contextual Awareness and Memory

To further enhance chatbot functionality, Groovy can be used to implement contextual awareness and memory. This feature allows the chatbot to remember previous interactions and maintain context during conversations.

3.1 Simple Memory Implementation

```groovy
def userMemory = [:] // Dictionary to store user data
def updateMemory(userId, key, value) {
```

```
userMemory[userId] = userMemory.getOrDefault(userId,
[:]) << [(key): value]
}
def recallMemory(userId, key) {
return    userMemory[userId]?.get(key)    ?:    "I    don't
remember that."
}
// Example usage
def userId = "user123"
updateMemory(userId, "lastOrder", "Order ID: 456")
println(recallMemory(userId, "lastOrder"))  //  Output:
"Order ID: 456"
```
```

In this snippet, we create a simple memory system where user interactions can be stored and recalled, allowing for a more personalized experience.

Groovy offers robust tools and capabilities for implementing conditional logic and dynamic responses in chatbot development. With its succinct syntax, support for closures, and integration with various frameworks, Groovy empowers developers to create intelligent conversational agents capable of handling complex interactions. As chatbots continue to play a vital role in customer engagement, utilizing Groovy for these tasks can lead to a more efficient and effective user experience. The versatility of Groovy not only simplifies the coding process but also significantly enhances the sophistication of chatbot interactions.
```

Building Modular and Reusable Code

This chapter will explore best practices for building modular and reusable code in Groovy, ensuring that your chatbot is not only functional but also adaptable and easy to maintain.

Understanding Modularity

Modularity refers to the practice of breaking down a large system into smaller, self-contained modules that can be developed, tested, and maintained independently. For chatbots, this could mean outlining various functionalities—such as user input processing, response generation, and integration with external APIs—into separate modules. The key benefits of modularity include:

Improved Readability: Smaller modules with a specific purpose are easier to read and understand.

Easier Testing: Isolated modules can be tested individually, making debugging simpler and more efficient.

Reuse of Components: Once a module has been developed, it can be reused in different projects without modification.

Structuring Your Groovy Project ### 1. Project Layout

To facilitate modularity, start by organizing your project structure. A typical Groovy project for a chatbot might look like this:

```
```

/chatbot-project

/src

/main

/groovy

/chatbot Chatbot.groovy

UserInputProcessor.groovy   ResponseGenerator.groovy
ApiIntegration.groovy Utils.groovy

/models

User.groovy

/resources config.properties

` ` `

In this structure:

Chatbot.groovy: The main class that orchestrates the chatbot's operations.

UserInputProcessor.groovy: Responsible   for
processing and validating user inputs.

ResponseGenerator.groovy: Generates appropriate responses based on user queries.

ApiIntegration.groovy: Manages connections to external services, such as databases or third-party APIs.

Utils.groovy: Contains utility functions, such as logging or common data transformations.

User.groovy: A model representing the user, encapsulating user-related data and methods.

2. Utilizing Groovy's Features

Groovy offers several features that can enhance modularity:

Grapes (Groovy's Dependency Management): Use

Grapes for managing external dependencies. This allows you to include libraries that can enhance functionality, like NLP (Natural Language Processing) libraries or database connectors.

Closures: Leveraging closures allows you to encapsulate behaviors and pass them around easily, promoting reuse across your modules.

```groovy
class ResponseGenerator {

def generateResponse(String userInput) { def responseHandler = { input ->

// Custom logic to determine the response based on input
return "You said: ${input}"

}

return responseHandler(userInput)

}

}
```

Traits: If multiple modules share common behaviors, consider using traits. Traits allow you to define reusable components that can be mixed into classes.

```groovy
trait Logging {

def log(String message) { println("${new Date()}: ${message}")
```

```groovy
    }
}

class UserInputProcessor implements Logging { void
processInput(String input) {

log("Processing input: ${input}")

// Input processing logic

    }
}
```
` ` `

Best Practices for Reusability

Building reusable code goes hand-in-hand with
modularity. Here are some best practices to follow in
Groovy:

1. Make Use of Interfaces and Abstract Classes

Defining interfaces for your components allows you to
swap out implementations easily. For instance, you could
have different response generation strategies depending
on the context of the chatbot or user preferences.

` ` `groovy

```groovy
interface ResponseStrategy {


String generateResponse(String input)
}

class SimpleResponseGenerator implements
ResponseStrategy { String generateResponse(String
input) {
```

```groovy
        return "That's interesting!"
    }
}

class        ComplexResponseGenerator        implements
ResponseStrategy   {   String   generateResponse(String
input) {
    // Complex NLP logic
    return "Let me think about that."
    }
}

// Usage

ResponseStrategy        strategy        =        new
SimpleResponseGenerator()
println(strategy.generateResponse("Hello"))
```

2. Configuration-Driven Development

Keep your implementations configurable rather than
hardcoding values. Use properties files for settings like
API endpoints, response templates, and other variables.
This makes it easier to adapt to changes without
modifying code.

```properties
# config.properties api.url=https://api.example.com
welcome.message=Welcome to our chatbot!
```

You can then load these values into your Groovy classes:

```groovy
def properties = new Properties()

properties.load(new
FileInputStream("src/resources/config.properties"))
println(properties.getProperty("welcome.message"))
```

3. Testing with Spock Framework

The Spock framework is a popular choice for unit testing Groovy code. Write tests for each module to verify functionality and ensure reliability. Regular testing alerts you to issues early, facilitating maintenance and enhancement.

```groovy
import spock.lang.Specification

class UserInputProcessorSpec extends Specification { def processor = new UserInputProcessor()


def "should log input when processed"() { expect:

processor.processInput("Hello") // Check logs manually or through assertions

}

}
```

Building modular and reusable code in Groovy for chatbots is not only beneficial but essential for long-term maintainability and flexibility. By structuring your project effectively, leveraging Groovy's features, adhering to best practices, and thoroughly testing your modules, you can create powerful chatbots that evolve as user needs change. With the right approach, your chatbot can be a robust solution, adaptable to various requirements without the necessity of rewriting code, ultimately leading to greater efficiency and a better user experience.

Conclusion

In this ultimate guide to Groovy programming for chatbots, we have journeyed through the intricacies of building intelligent chatbots that can elevate user interactions and provide meaningful, real-time engagements. As we reach the conclusion of this guide, it's essential to reflect on the knowledge and insights acquired throughout our exploration.

We began our journey by understanding Groovy's strengths as a dynamic language, emphasizing its simplicity and versatility. The unique features of Groovy have made it a powerful choice for chatbot development. From its seamless integration with Java to its concise syntax, Groovy allows developers to craft efficient and maintainable code that empowers chatbots to perform complex tasks while remaining user-friendly.

Through various chapters, we delved into the foundational concepts of chatbot architecture, natural language processing, and machine learning integrations. We armed ourselves with the tools necessary to build chatbots that not only understand user queries but also respond intelligently and contextually. From utilizing popular frameworks like Grails and Spring to leveraging libraries for NLP and AI, this guide has equipped you with the skills to create sophisticated conversational agents.

Moreover, we explored best practices for chatbot design, ensuring that your application not only functions well but also provides a delightful user experience. We discussed the importance of empathy in conversations and how to structure dialogues that feel natural and engaging.

As you embark on your journey to create your own chatbots, remember that the learning doesn't stop here. The world of technology and artificial intelligence is always evolving, and staying updated with the latest developments will empower you to refine your bots and explore new possibilities. Don't hesitate to experiment, iterate, and innovate as you navigate the landscape of chatbot development.

We hope this guide has inspired you to harness the power of Groovy in building intelligent chatbots that can resonate with users and address their needs. The future is bright for those who dare to explore the realms of AI and conversational interfaces, and with Groovy by your side, you are well-equipped to lead the charge.

Thank you for joining us on this enlightening journey. We wish you the best of luck in your chatbot endeavors and look forward to seeing the incredible creations you will develop. Happy coding!

Biography

Davis Simon is a passionate software developer, seasoned backend architect, and advocate for clean, efficient code. With over a decade of experience in web application development, Davis has built scalable, high-performing systems for startups and enterprises alike. His expertise lies in backend development and leveraging the power of languages like Groovy to create APIs and microservices that are as robust as they are elegant.

A self-proclaimed "Groovy enthusiast," Davis discovered the language early in his career and quickly fell in love with its versatility and simplicity. His dedication to Groovy programming inspired him to write this book and share his insights with aspiring developers looking to harness its potential for backend development.

When he's not writing code or crafting the next big web application, Davis enjoys exploring emerging technologies, mentoring new developers, and experimenting with creative ways to solve programming challenges. Outside of the tech world, Davis is an avid gamer and a lover of all things sci-fi, often finding inspiration for his projects in futuristic tales and virtual worlds.

With this eBook, Davis invites you to join him on a journey to revolutionize backend development with Groovy. His approachable teaching style and practical advice will empower you to take your skills to the next level—whether you're building your first API or architecting complex systems.

Glossary: Groovy Programming language for Chatbots

A

Abstraction: A fundamental concept in programming that refers to the simplification of complex systems by reducing the details to the necessary elements. In chatbot development, abstraction allows developers to create high-level interfaces for various functionalities without getting bogged down by the underlying implementation details.

B

Bot Framework: A set of tools and libraries that simplifies the process of building chatbots. Groovy can be integrated into several bot frameworks, enabling developers to leverage its concise syntax while creating rich conversational experiences.

C

Closure: A feature in Groovy that allows you to define a block of code that can be executed later. Closures are particularly useful in chatbots for handling callbacks, event listeners, and managing asynchronous operations.

Chatbot: A software application designed to simulate human conversation, either through text or voice interactions. Groovy provides a robust framework for building chatbots by utilizing its dynamic capabilities and extensive libraries.

D

Dynamic Typing: A characteristic of Groovy that allows variables to hold different types of values over their lifecycle. This flexibility enables developers to write more concise and readable code, which is particularly advantageous in chatbot development where data can vary significantly.

E

Event-Driven Programming: A programming paradigm that emphasizes the responding to user actions and events. In chatbot development, Groovy's support for event-driven programming allows bots to handle user inputs efficiently and provide timely responses.

F

Framework: A structure that provides a foundation for building software applications. In the context of Groovy and chatbots, frameworks like Grails or Spring Boot can be used to streamline the development process and enhance scalability.

G

Groovy: An agile and dynamic programming language that enhances the Java platform. It boasts a syntax that is easier and more expressive than Java, making it an ideal choice for developers creating interactive applications like chatbots.

H

Handling User Input: The process of capturing and processing text or voice commands from users. Utilizing Groovy's string manipulation and pattern matching capabilities simplifies the implementation of natural language processing in chatbots.

I

Integration: The process of connecting different software systems or components. Groovy's compatibility with Java libraries and APIs allows for easy integration with third-party chatbot platforms, databases, and messaging services like Slack or Facebook Messenger.

J

JVM (Java Virtual Machine): A runtime environment that allows Java (and Groovy) applications to run on various platforms. Understanding the JVM is crucial for optimizing Groovy applications for performance and portability.

K

Keyword: A reserved word in Groovy that has a special meaning and cannot be used as an identifier (such as variable names). Example keywords include `def`, `class`, and `void`, which are essential for defining structures in Groovy chatbot programs.

L

Library: A collection of pre-written code that developers can use to perform common tasks. Groovy has access to a plethora of Java libraries, which means developers can leverage existing tools for functionalities like HTTP requests and JSON parsing when building chatbots.

M

Message Handling: The process of interpreting and

responding to messages from users. Groovy facilitates efficient message handling through its concise and expressive syntax, allowing for the quick development of complex decision-making algorithms in chatbots.

N

Natural Language Processing (NLP): A branch of artificial intelligence that focuses on the interaction between computers and humans through natural language. Groovy can be paired with NLP libraries to enhance chatbots' abilities to understand and interpret user intent.

O

Object-Oriented Programming (OOP): A programming paradigm that organizes software design around data, or objects, rather than functions and logic. Groovy supports OOP principles, making it easy to create reusable components for chatbot applications.

P

Platform Independence: The ability of software to run on various operating systems without modification. Groovy's design, being compatible with the JVM, ensures chatbots can be deployed across different environments seamlessly.

Q

Query: A request for information. In chatbot functionality, queries are often made to databases or external services to gain insights or retrieve data needed for conversations.

R

RESTful API: An architectural style that defines a set of constraints for creating web services. Groovy's ease of creating RESTful APIs makes it a powerful tool for chatbots that need to interact with web services.

S

Scripting: Writing short programs or scripts to automate tasks within a chatbot. Groovy's scripting capabilities allow for rapid development and testing of chatbot features.

T

Testing: The process of evaluating a chatbot to ensure it functions as expected. Groovy's support for testing frameworks, like Spock, facilitates thorough testing of chatbot interactions and business logic.

U

User Experience (UX): The overall experience a user has when interacting with a chatbot. Effective design and implementation in Groovy can greatly enhance the UX by making conversations more intuitive and engaging.

V

Variable: A storage location identified by a name that holds data which can be changed during program execution. Groovy allows for a wide variety of variable types, which can help manage user data and context in chatbots efficiently.

W

Webhook: A method for one application to send real-time data to another when an event occurs. In chatbots, Groovy can easily handle webhooks to receive and process information from external services.

X, Y, Z

While specific terms for these letters may be less common in Groovy or chatbot development, they could encompass concepts like **XML** (an example of data format often used in web services) and

Yielding (in the context of coroutine-like behavior in asynchronous programming).

www.ingramcontent.com/pod-product-compliance
Lightning Source LLC
Chambersburg PA
CBHW070946050326
40689CB00014B/3362

* 9 7 9 8 3 0 6 6 8 2 0 5 1 *